# Table of Contents

# Table of Contents

# Table of Contents

# Foreword

The WorkForce Center (WFC) in south Minneapolis is one of the busiest in the state. In a neighborhood rich in ethnic restaurants and with a huge "global" indoor market just a short walk away, the WFC's diverse population visits every day to use computers and speak to job counselors in a large and open room, partly illuminated by the glow of monitors revealing job-seeking websites.

The south Minneapolis WFC serves thousands of job seekers annually. The first-floor crowd mainly works the Web. The story is different upstairs where, in a training room, at least 30 people patiently sat through a presentation on how to create a resume.

They range in age from their 20s and up. For some, the work of finding a job is a familiar situation, something they face every few years in a fast-changing job market.

For others, it was a new challenge, and they need to learn how to develop a resume and other assets that could eventually land them employment. One man, in the back of the room, turned out to be employed but took the class "just in case" he was laid off, representing a certain nervousness felt by many American workers in an unsettled era.

Welcome to the job market of the 21st century. "The average American today will work in five to eight fields and have an average of 18 jobs over a period of 40 to 60 years of their work life," says Paul Sears, a job counselor specialist in the south Minneapolis WFC. As companies shed jobs or change their production processes, others bulk up and hire. Having the right skills and attitude, says Sears, will help job seekers find new jobs, but they may have to change careers more than once — or twice, or three times.

In the training room, the participants share one singular desire: a job. And the resume class will help inform them of what employers want and expect as they describe their work lives on a one- or two-page document, along with a cover letter that they hope will draw the attention of managers assigned to hire new employees.

The other classes will give participants tips on finding hidden job markets, resumes, networking, researching companies, Internet job search strategies, interviews, thank you letters and other job-seeking skills. If you could not make the classes — and we highly suggest you sign up — you are lucky in one regard: You hold in your hands the book the WFC presenters use to guide participants through an extraordinary amount of information.

South Minneapolis operates just like Minnesota's other WorkForce Centers. Collectively, the employees of these centers are charged with the important duty of assisting Minnesotans in finding jobs. And one of the key assets they have used for more than two decades is "Creative Job Search" (CJS).

Since 1994, CJS has sold more than 15,500 copies not just in Minnesota but all over the United States, Europe, Australia and elsewhere. This edition covers several significant areas: career planning, finding a job when you are in the 50-plus age group and the importance of social media in finding a job.

While CJS has plenty of Minnesota examples and resources, it also boasts information that will be relevant to readers in Richmond, Va., or even Rio de Janeiro. The core tools and skills in finding employment are borderless. We hope you find this book helpful in your quest and, more to the point, we hope it leads to a good job for you in the future.

Finally, we would like to thank the subject experts and many other people who were involved in the writing, editing, and layout and design of this book. It was truly a collaborative effort.

We like to think that in this new edition we offer a menu of strategies, tactics and tools for a new age of job hunting.

# CHAPTER 1

# Career Planning

*"Nobody can go back and start a new beginning, but anyone can start today and make a new ending."*

— MARIA ROBINSON, WRITER

What are you going to do with the rest of your life? That's a good question to ponder at any age. It's probably on your mind if you are reading this book, attending a job search class or in a job that you don't like but cannot afford to leave — just yet. If you are unemployed you have some decisions to make, especially if you work in a career where the opportunities are diminishing and the road ahead looks bleak.

It's a good question, too, if you're a college graduate or a 30-something worker who isn't sure your career is headed in the right direction. It may be time for a change. Planning should even be embraced by job seekers who like their careers but may need to more sharply focus on where they want to go in their next jobs. After all, the career you have today could end in five years and you might have to shift to a new profession.

Robert Reich, former United States secretary of labor and current University of California at Berkeley economics professor, once had this to say about careers: "There are no longer career paths … Careers paths are gone. They're not even trails. They're not even horse paths."

That's a bit of an exaggeration, of course, since career ladders still exist, though not nearly as many people spend enough time at any one firm — or in one profession — to climb them. And some careers are declining as they are offshored to India, China, Mexico and other countries. Even information technology jobs have been impacted by the offshoring trend.

Career planning is the kind of issue that drives job seekers crazy. When do you know when to leave a career? It's like the old Clash song: "Should I Stay or Should I Go." Should you "recareer" or continue to look for opportunities in your field? Should you start your own business? The answers to those questions belong to you. We'll try to address some of those issues in this chapter to help you decide what comes next.

# A JOB NO MORE

People who have lost their jobs potentially face significant emotional, psychological, financial and physical challenges. It is an unpleasant and difficult predicament, a trap door to anger and resentment, outrage and depression. To add to the injury, the jobless invariably face a bevy of insensitive assessments ("These things happen for a reason.") to time-worn clichés such as "I'm sure something better will come along."

Job loss can impact nearly every aspect of a person's life, from spending habits to self-esteem. Job loss can make people stronger, meeker, energized or demoralized. It can turn job seekers into small-business owners or consultants. It can spark ambition or extinguish it. And how anyone will handle a job loss cannot be always predicted. Most people will need some time to bounce back.

## Managing Emotions and Psychological Stress

There's no doubt, regardless of whether you loved or hated your job, you will feel its loss. Lynn Joseph, the author of "The Job-Loss Recovery Guide" and manager of www.joblossrecovery.com, sees the following as constants following job loss: shock and denial, fear and anxiety, anger, bargaining, depression, acceptance and closure.

Joseph told The Washington Post she suggests a four-part process. First, "recognize your true feelings" and the anger inside you. Second, look for a safe outlet. Write your thoughts down. "Writing for 20 minutes a day over six days has been scientifically shown to lead to reframing difficult situations like job loss, new insights and even to landing a job sooner." Third, search for a sense of forgiveness, of yourself, or your former employer. You need not express it to your former boss, for example, but you must feel it in yourself. Fourth, change is going to come. The first three steps will lead to a better sense of yourself and prepare you for the work world again.

## Financial Aspects of Unemployment

You will need to get your financial house in order. Minnesotans can find out how to apply for unemployment benefits by logging onto www.uimn.org. Residents of other states can visit www.careeronestop.org/reemployment for information about unemployment insurance. If applicable, try to get health coverage through your spouse's employer or your parents. If that is not an option, sign up for COBRA (the Consolidated Omnibus Budget Reconciliation Act), which allows you to pay group rates for health insurance for a limited time. Be prepared for added expenses because you will be paying the full cost of the insurance without any funding from your former employer if your COBRA ends or if you do not have the option for COBRA coverage. Or visit mnsure.org, Minnesota's online health exchange that was launched in September 2013. The website is part of the federal law requiring virtually all U.S. adults to carry health insurance or pay a penalty.

Using MNsure, you can search for health insurance options according to ZIP code and other criteria. The federal government website is healthcare.gov.

Should you receive a severance package, use it carefully. You have no idea how long you will remain unemployed. The key is to budget your money. What do you need to live? How much does your mortgage, rent, food, entertainment and transportation cost? What can you live without? The reality of your situation may force some hard choices about getting rid of certain expenses such as top tier cable television, eating out three times a week, going to movies or attending concerts and plays.

A strategy going forward is to cut extraneous costs early on just in case unemployment lasts longer than you assumed. The Web has excellent budgeting tools available for free or for relatively affordable subscriptions. Miranda Marquit in GoodFinancialcents.com suggests that Mint, BudgetPulse, Buxfer and Moneytrackin' are among the best online budgeting tools. Many of these financial tools can be accessed anywhere and anytime with an app for your smartphone.

## Physical Challenges

Unemployment can create health issues. Laid-off workers are 54 percent more likely than those continuously employed to have fair or poor health and 83 percent more likely to develop a stress related condition such as stroke, heart attack, heart disease or arthritis.

How can you avoid that? Build in an exercise regimen. Of all the expenses you may have, try to keep the health club membership. Or, use local recreation centers and the great outdoors to keep your body in shape. The tendency of job seekers is to surf the Web for any potential jobs, make networking calls, attend networking meetings and then find time to get in some exercise. Experts suggest setting that exercise time into your schedule early since it will help you deal with the stress and disillusionment of unemployment while preparing your mind and body for the rigors of job hunting.

## A CAREER PLANNING GAME PLAN

Planning your next move demands self-examination and research before setting a job goal. Maybe you want to be a famous actor or a pop star? Go for it, but have a backup plan. If you're looking at a less risky career choice it may be time to look at what you've done and where you'd like to go and what you need to do to get there before starting the next chapter of your career.

The literature on career planning generally agrees on a multi-step process to get people moving toward goals. Everyone has different experiences, desires and timelines. Yet a disorganized approach, for sure, will lead to frustration and disappointment rather than a focus on a new career. During this section we will reference other parts of this book since the principles of any job search remain largely the same, whether you're anxiously starting a different profession or staying in the same one.

## Step One: Let's Talk About You

One simple step you can take in this direction is conducting a self-assessment. You can do this at one of Minnesota's WorkForce Centers through our employment counselors or through online assessment tests available at www. iseek.org, careeronestop, MySkillsMyFuture and other websites. The information gleaned from the test may put a damper on your plans to become an astronaut, but you may find some hidden skills and talents — leadership, communicating, working with tools, whatever — that will unlock ideas for new careers.

Job experts believe a good assessment includes interests, skills, values, preferred environments, temperament, motivations, work experience, training needs, and your current work and financial status. These areas give definition to your career search. Do you want a job with great regularity and little change, one with or without travel, with a large company, or a small one? Where creativity is rewarded? Or where doing diligently many of the same tasks daily is celebrated? Can you afford a new career? These are just some questions you will want to answer prior to thinking about heading in a new direction.

Avoid diminishing your creative impulse by placing too many limitations on it. "Don't let yourself get stuck in 'I can't do this, I can't do that' kinds of thinking that reflect only current real-world constraints but not what could be developed," argues Leonard Lang, a Minneapolis-based career coach and author of "Guide to Lifework: Working with Integrity and Heart." "By thinking creatively, you can be re-energized and find new solutions you hadn't dreamed of before. But that won't happen if you get stuck on thinking first of these constraints, such as there are bills to pay … kids are in school … 'I don't have the education.' Dealing with those constraints is vital after you get a vision of your career."

## Time for Homework

Armed with a greater sense of yourself through personal and professional assessments, you now have to begin a major research project. Later in this book, we show many places on the Web and at the library where you can explore careers that you find appealing and that may fit your skill set — or your skill set with additional training.

Follow a strategy of studying the demand for occupations you find attractive. You will be advised to "follow your bliss" in career books and on the Web. That's an option — maybe you could find a career transforming your skills as an amateur taxidermist into a professional one. Just don't make the decision blindly. Understand that a new career may sometimes entail considerable financial sacrifice.

By doing your homework, you might want to consider a career in the top 20 or 30 growing professions rather than strike out on an unlikely dream of becoming, well, a brain surgeon at age 55. No career counselor wants to dampen enthusiasm, but a dose of reality is often required unless a person really possesses the absolute drive and determination to take on an exceptionally challenging profession.

One job expert related the story of a woman who really did want to become a physician at age 40 and understood the sacrifices and time it would take to embark upon a medical career. She went with her passion. That's an extraordinary story, and a rare one. More commonplace are people who develop skills in one area that they can repurpose in another field.

Rather than rehash a later chapter of this book, we will refer you to Chapter 2 for details on occupations, conducting labor market surveys, reaching out for informational interviews and finding job survey data.

## Filling Skill Gaps

Once you have a pretty good idea of what career or careers you want to pursue, you may find your lack of knowledge or skills will make it hard for you to find employment. Let's say you sold medical products to hospitals for a number of years and want to transition into a role where you're a care provider, such as Licensed Practical Nurse or Registered Nurse. You will need additional schooling in order to make that dramatic a leap.

Perhaps you seek a different career path in the same or a similar profession. A programmer who wants to get into management could consider a master's of business degree or a leadership/executive training program at a local college. That programmer could volunteer for managerial-style jobs with an IT association to experience, in a small way, the skills demanded of a larger managerial position in the future.

You can, in effect, conduct your own "skill gap analysis" to determine what education, degrees and training — or combination of all three — might be needed in a different career. Then you need to find the education or training you require for your new career, an issue less of a problem in large or medium-sized cities where many colleges and private institutions have created night and weekend courses and degrees for working adults. (If you're unemployed you may qualify for financial assistance and be able to attend day classes. You might also wish to explore online education and adult learning opportunities.)

## Making a Move

You may decide, in the end, to stay in your current profession or to take whatever positions come your way, a strategy not without appeal in a changing economy. You could come to the conclusion that you'd prefer your favorite activities remain hobbies instead of potentially new careers or that you devote your ancillary talents to volunteer organizations instead of professional, paying positions.

More than a few brilliant amateur photographers have not opened studios, for instance, and many great teachers remain mentors and tutors at schools and have not gone into the profession. Your talents beyond work always can be exercised in other avenues.

In many cases staying in your field will be a wise choice. Not everyone can, or should, start a new career. The question you have to answer in moving in a different direction is whether you can continue in your profession. Can you still find a job or contract work? And if you're starting anew, do you have the commitment and resilience required to make what will be a monumental change fraught with the potential for considerable setbacks, roadblocks, challenges and struggles?

Career coach Leonard Lang suggests people test drive their vision. Take a course or two in the career you want to pursue, rather than entering a full-time degree program. A few courses later you might decide that teaching elementary school isn't something you want to do, after all. Or, you find your commitment has solidified and to save time you're going to become a full-time student. Investing time in courses or training will give you a clearer picture of whether a new career is what you really want.

If you have to take a temporary job while retraining or preparing for a new profession, "this is nothing to feel bad about," adds Lang,

## CASE STUDY:

### MARY BETH HEFFERNAN'S TRANSITION FROM VOLUNTEER TO EMPLOYEE

**Road-weary from spending** as many as four months a year on the road and looking for a chance to spend more time with her two children, Mary Beth Heffernan decided to take a break from corporate America.

After having spent 18 years building a global footprint for a Twin Cities biomedical company, she went home to two young children and to volunteer. She signed on to help Second Harvest, a local food shelf, starting as an envelope stuffer and then moving up to managing groups that came to pack groceries for food shelves.

For more than a year Heffernan enjoyed contributing to an organization committed to helping others in their time of need. After hinting that she might be interested in actually working for Second Harvest, an executive interviewed her for the job of donor relations manager.

She joined Second Harvest in 2008, this time as an employee. "The pieces fell together for me during the 14 months I was off," says Heffernan. "I told the people who interviewed me I was looking to work in a nonprofit. It's less frantic than working for a public company, where you have to meet your goals quarterly, but there are more deadlines because there is more to do with fewer people."

who has spoken at Minnesota WorkForce Centers. "It may be that a transitional job will give you experience or connections that help you move toward your larger goal."

If you take the plunge into a new career, you will not be alone. A Minnesota newspaper highlighted many career changers, among them an airline mechanic studying to become a biomedical technician, a project manager who opened a consignment store, a used car dealer who sells his own homemade salsa at area grocery stores and farmers markets, a former assistant principal taking classes to become a computer technician and a recruiter at a large national retail chain who left that job to pursue a singing career.

## THE PATH OF INDEPENDENCE

For many job seekers a return to the 9 to 5 existence, even in a new profession, fails to excite the imagination or to create a firm desire to move in that direction. Many people may like their professions but simply no longer want a boss, or to work for others. The jobs in their field may have dried up even if the work has not. They may be ready to become "consultants" or "independent contractors" or work solo or with small groups of other individuals on projects.

Thousands of people earn a living in Minnesota as independent contractors. Some of them team up to create small agencies and businesses;

others prefer to remain on their own. Several professions lend themselves to an independent approach, among them marketing, public relations, advertising, journalism (or freelance/contract writing), information technology, architecture, technical writing, home building and repair, plumbing, law and research. In whatever profession you're in, there's a good chance your company has used or is employing contractors who have their own business.

Independent contractors face many challenges. They have to market their own products and services, network constantly, cold call if necessary, and meet and exceed client expectations on a routine basis because of — usually — stiff competition from other contractors. Turn in bad work and you will get no more work. If an employee is struggling, managers generally provide them counseling, training and a second chance. They have no obligation to provide that to independent contractors and generally will not unless the parties have had a long established relationship. Great devotion to clients is often necessary.

There are other issues. Contractors and small-business owners have to pay for their own medical insurance, a huge cost center. Other benefits common in full-time employment — disability insurance, pre-tax deductions, 401(k)s and other retirement vehicles — must be self-funded. You're on your own. Services such as accounting and contracting must be done in-house or handled by another firm. The responsibilities are much greater than working for someone else.

So what are the advantages? Ask any small-business owner or contractor and they will probably speak to the issue of freedom, the upside in some professions of a significantly higher income than a paid position, fewer limitations on vacation or sick time, greater flexibility in raising a family (or indulging in other non-work interests) and a much wider variety of work. There is an indescribable sensation of achievement in earning every dollar of your income through your own effort, from finding clients to completing a project to maintaining good client relationships.

It has been called the American dream. And for millions of Americans, it is a dream come true. No longer are contractors "between opportunities" and dismissed as tiny players in a big economy. They are the largest job generation machine in the United States and will continue to be in the 21st century. Still, running any kind of business demands a high level of ambition, risk tolerance, attention to detail and professional skill.

This dream is not for everyone, nor should it be. Starting a small business, however, may become one of the few options left for job seekers, especially those in the later stages of their careers. And it remains a way for people to create their own careers and achieve a finer work-life balance instead of having their fate determined by the whims of employers.

## Living With the Decision

You will have to live with your decision for some time, so make it wisely. Once you have committed to a new direction, stay the course for a while because success will not happen overnight, or even after a year. It's likely to take a while to earn a degree, absorb training or sell your product or services. Then, it will take time to find the employment you seek.

If an opportunity arises in your former profession, it may leave you at a crossroads. Whether to take the offer presents a dilemma, especially if you miss your former work. Should you recall that work with a significant anxiousness and dread, you will want to take great consideration prior to making a decision. Can you live with going back, especially if you need the money? Or is it better to soldier on?

Most career changers will never have that option since they cease sending out resumes and looking in their fields. Others may entertain a few phone calls with offers. And then they'll have to decide whether to continue the new plan or retrench and head back to the comfort of a job and a career they once knew.

# NOTES

# CHAPTER 2

# Preparing for the Job Hunt

*"Woke up, fell out of bed, dragged a comb across my head, found my way downstairs and drank a cup …"*

—"A DAY IN THE LIFE," JOHN LENNON AND PAUL McCARTNEY

The Beatles may have been singing of the life of an average day of a typical British worker circa late 1960s, but if you're a job seeker take heed: You, too, need to get out of bed, have a cup and hit the computer and the phone to continue your search. A successful job search requires organization, effort and self-discipline.

If you are used to having someone else organize your activities, you will be mastering new skills that will require you to stay focused, avoid distractions and stay the course, despite potentially rough waters on the voyage to employment. Start with a few good habits and practices right away to avoid getting caught in a cycle where you fritter away time without any attempt to keep yourself focused and accountable to the goal of finding a job.

## GETTING ORGANIZED

A successful job search requires effort. That means getting organized, scheduling time for tasks and keeping a record of your achievements or mileposts ("made seven cold calls today," "had an informational interview").

### Managing a Schedule

Successful job seekers have mastered the art of managing their schedules and establishing measurable goals. For example, commit a block of hours every day for searching and identifying companies you want to contact and jobs you want to apply for. Consider a schedule in which every Monday morning you conduct Internet searches that at minimum result in the names of 10 new employers. Tuesday's goal could be contacting the 10 employers you identified Monday. Tuesday morning might be a good time to reach employers, from 9 to 11 a.m., for example.

You should set some goals for your search. The toughest thing about being unemployed is the lack of accountability to anyone but yourself. That's why joining a networking group or reporting progress to a friend, spouse or partner makes certain sense. It's relatively easy to get sidetracked during a job search by spending valuable hours surfing the Internet. Strange curiosities and searches that take you into informational netherworlds can consume endless hours. Filling an eight-hour work day without a job can be remarkably easy. Remember the sports proverb: Keep your eye on the ball.

Of course, all work and no play will make for irritability. If you have reached out to 20 employers during a week and had a few networking events and interviews, offer yourself a reward involving your passions or interests. A movie. A walk in the park. An afternoon at a museum. And then start the search anew.

## Keeping Records

During the job-search process you may make hundreds of contacts and generate new opportunities for part-time and full-time work. You need to maintain a filing system to organize your progress. A variety of systems are available including computer filing systems, alphabetized three-ring binders, notebooks or mobile devices. Choose the system that makes the most sense to you.

A "contact tracker," as some job experts call it, will assist in creating a database of people and companies you have called, emailed and sent your resume and cover letter during a search. Keep records of when you make contacts, who you called, their emails, addresses and websites. Just because a company turned you down doesn't mean it won't become a prospect in the future. A general rule in sales is that it takes at least three contacts to turn a prospect into a client. That may not be true when seeking a position with a company: Hitting them half a dozen times with phone calls and letters may not work at all. Or, you may be working for that company someday soon.

The resumes you send out will require follow-up calls and the networking and informational calls you make to potential employers will create the need to send out resumes, which in turn, will generate more follow-up calls. Without using career management tracking mechanisms it would be very easy to get lost in the details and inadvertently let important opportunities fall through the cracks. Here's a list of tools to help you track your progress online: http://workawesome.com/goals/online-goal-tracking-tools/.

## RESEARCHING EMPLOYERS

Now that you have an idea for organizing your job search you can begin conducting research in order to find openings and employers you seek to work for in the future. By researching an industry, occupation or employer, you gain a better understanding of job availability, company culture, potential growth of businesses and industries, and how your skills could be applied to a different profession, if that becomes a necessity.

Finding out about potential employers gives you a chance to measure your qualifications against those required by a particular company. They force you to determine whether you need more training in a certain area and whether the skills you have match the talent employers want.

## Structuring Research

When beginning your research, start gathering information on specific occupations, industries, individual companies and job availability in your area. Your research will naturally become more specific as you gain momentum. Company websites, career information resources, trade journals and online job boards are all good resources for discovering what experience, training and knowledge are required by employers.

Create an online or paper filing system containing research pertaining to companies you want to reach. That way, you don't have to rely on Google every time you want to look over the content you found last week on the target of your research. Sometimes articles mysteriously disappear or land much further down the list of hits on search engines; better to print it out, send a copy to your email account or cut and paste content into a Word document.

What should you look for? Study a company's products or services, size, history, location(s) (especially in relationship to where you live), mission statement or philosophy (or "value proposition" if such a document exists) and financial situation, as well as potential for growth. You should dig a little deeper and find out what changes the employer has undergone in the last five years and what kind of human resource policies it has, from flex time to a commitment to provide community services.

Finally, read local media stories on technology and updates and events on new or expanding businesses. Think plant expansions, new product roll-outs, or sponsorship of events, which are potentially great information for job seekers. An expanding workforce may show up in a press release but not in local wanted ads.

The same information will make you look good should you get an interview in which you can show how well-informed you are by saying, "I noticed you're opening a new plant in Kentucky …" or "I'm really intrigued by that new product you released, the biodegradable coffee cup …" Companies not only appreciate that you found them through diligent research, they are equally impressed when you display knowledge of their recent actions and address issues within their industries.

## Labor Market Survey

Labor market surveys are tools that can help determine if an occupation or specific line of work is appropriate for you. Labor market surveys can be effective because they can help you gain insights into fields and occupations.

## RESOURCES FOR RESEARCH

Listed below are some of the many resources that have information about employers.

- Minnesota WorkForce Center Resource Area staff or staff at your local state employment service

- People working with the employer

- Current newspapers, trade journals and business magazines and newspapers. (In the Twin Cities, Finance and Commerce and The Business Journal are good examples of publications with stories about growing employers.)

- Employer websites

- Articles in Internet publications containing information that relates to industries, occupations or employers

- Social networking services, blogs and company employee sites (Some independent employee sites are interesting because they offer insights not found on "official" employer sites.)

- Libraries, which have special sections on occupations, careers and job search information, article databases, business publications, business directories and other resources

- College placement offices and alumni associations

- Chamber of Commerce or Jaycees

- Annual reports

- Employer newsletters and brochures available from the employer's public relations office or human resources department

The pace of business is so fast today that calling people and asking questions about their occupations may result in few call-backs or answered emails. The Internet has voluminous amounts of information on careers, potential job openings in those occupations and even reflections or articles by bloggers, journalists and others that describe what it is like to work in a field. Many job search books have suggestions on doing a labor market survey even though it seems unlikely, given the pressures of an average workday, that many people have the time to answer a series of questions from someone they have never met.

If you want to conduct a labor market survey, try to keep it in your network of contacts so you at least have an opening when making that call: "Jim Schmidt told me to give you a call. I'm interested in working at 3M and want to learn more about the company's culture," sounds better than "I want to work at 3M. Can you tell me what it's like to work there?"

Be clear, be precise, tell the individual you will not take up more than a few minutes of his or her time and hope for a return call. Keep in mind not everyone will tell the truth about an employer to a total stranger, even one recommended by a friend. You may gain some insights or you might find the practice of labor market surveys a waste of time in an age when so much information about companies is widely available on the Internet and at your local library.

## A Deeper Data Dive

If you know the specific occupation or line of work that interests you, consult the Occupational Information Network (O*Net) or the Bureau of Labor Statistics websites (www.bls.gov). Other reference books are available at Minnesota WorkForce Centers or your local state employment office, public libraries, technical schools, colleges and universities.

Libraries are a great place to access databases that may not be available for free on the Internet. In Minnesota anyone with a library card can register with the Hennepin County Public Library system and then access its vast repository of online databases. Other library systems may have similar arrangements. The following are among the best business databases:

- **Business Insights: Essentials:** Research and compare companies and industries using industry rankings, company profiles, market share data, investment reports, charts, graphs and more.

- **Business Source Premier:** The database holds economic data, company profiles, industry information, market research reports and much more.

- **ELM:** Electronic Library for Minnesota is an online virtual library specifically for Minnesota residents. It contains full-text magazine, newspaper, and reference articles, as well as videos, images, and information from encyclopedias, almanacs, directories and other information resources. You can use ELM from home, work, school or any place that has Internet access.

- **ReferenceUSA:** The directory of U.S.-based businesses provides a way to search by business name, industry, city county and ZIP code while offering a panoply of information.

These databases are available online, too, but the fees charged for their use is often substantial. That's why it's better to physically go to the library to use them or to register so you can gain Web access with a library card.

You can also tap into social networking sites for content on jobs. In that setting there may be members of networking groups willing to offer you insights into a particular field. Networking groups in an occupation such as project management or medical technology or communications are great settings in which to glean insider knowledge and observations of what is required of practitioners in that industry, training, openings, salaries and so forth.

## LABOR MARKET SURVEY SOURCES

- Minnesota Department of Employment and Economic Development, Research and Statistics Labor Market Information Help Line at 651.259.7384, or email (deed.lmi@state.mn.us)

- ISEEK (www.iseek.org), a Minnesota-based job information site with posted openings

- CareerOneStop (www.careeronestop.org)

- Bureau of Labor Statistics (www.bls.gov)

- Occupational Information Network (O*Net) (online.onetcenter.org)

- Hoover's Online (www.hoovers.com) or Vault (www.vault.com) are go-to sites for larger publicly (and privately) traded companies

## SMALLER MARKET RESEARCH

If you live in a small or medium-sized city, the kind of extensive research described in this chapter may not be all that relevant. You probably know a lot about the major employers, and the smaller ones are not going to be part of any of the national databases found on the Web or in libraries. Where does that leave you?

The best basic research you can do is to get the names of small employers, study their websites and see if they list jobs. Should the management team be listed, take a look and see if you recognize any names. In a small town they may be members of your church or have children at your school. Even if you don't know them, try to call or email them. Chances are they probably have a little more time to chat with a job seeker than their larger corporate counterparts.

You can also employ something as simple as your local phone book (in print or online versions). Look at the companies in your profession, or a profession you seek to join, and take down their names, addresses and phone numbers. If your community's phone number provider has an online directory, use that because companies listed sometimes have a link directly to their website — if they have one.

Another research source is the website of your local newspaper and the closest regional daily newspaper. At those sites you can usually do searches of companies and see what stories have been written about them. Even smaller firms, if they are growing or offer intriguing products and services, may have had articles written about them.

Since many small dailies and weeklies don't have extensive archives on the Web, you will have to go to your local library to search for copies or, alternatively, call the newspaper itself. Many of them file stories by subject matter and are willing to share those with local residents as long as they don't take them from the premises.

Minnesota has two fine resources for job seekers, noted earlier, in MinnesotaWorks.net and www.iseek.org. You can look for positions through a ZIP code search and let the search engine know how many miles you are willing to commute. Depending on where you live you may have to extend the search out to find the kind of job you desire.

Finally, the best research for job seekers in smaller communities comes in networking with friends, family, neighbors and other acquaintances. Great research, especially on smaller employers, just isn't available. That's where cold-calling — dealt with in Chapter 6 — and networking will be exceptionally important to your research. In the yin and yang of job hunting, smaller markets have the same advantage and disadvantage: a limited number of employers that you will have to research and contact, yet a smaller number of available jobs.

# ENDNOTES

| Time | Sunday | Monday | Tuesday | Wednesday | Thursday | Friday | Saturday |
|---|---|---|---|---|---|---|---|
| **JOB SEARCH SCHEDULE SAMPLE** — Week of September 7 | | | | | | | |
| **8:00 a.m.** | Shower and dress. Read the newspaper. | Shower and dress by 8:30. Set goals for the day/week. | Same as Monday. | Same as Monday. | Same as Monday. | Same as Monday. | Go to the farmers market. |
| **9:00 a.m.** | Read Sunday paper. Check online for newspaper job ads by 9:30. | Respond by phone to Sunday ads. | Make networking calls. | Return calls. Schedule appointments. | Attend job club. | Return calls. Schedule appointments. | |
| **10:00 a.m.** | Take a walk, play with the kids, etc. | Get information for writing responses to ads. Go to the Minnesota WorkForce Center. | Make networking calls. | Attend job fair. | Attend job club. | Make networking calls. | |
| **11:00 a.m.** | Have some fun! | Write cover letters. Make changes on resume. | Return phone calls. Schedule appointments. | | Do informational interview. | | |
| **12:00 p.m.** | Lunch | Lunch | Lunch | Lunch | Lunch | Lunch | Lunch |
| **1:00 p.m.** | | Appointment | Appointment | Check out Minnesota WorkForce Center computer. | Appointment | Research the employer for the interview next week. | |
| **2:00 p.m.** | | Appointment | Appointment | Call on leads obtained at Minnesota WorkForce Center. | Appointment | Research the employer for the interview next week. | |
| **3:00 p.m.** | | Appointment | Appointment | Appointment | | Research the employer for the interview next week. | |
| **4:00 p.m.** | | Walk | Walk | Walk | Walk | Walk | |
| **5:00 p.m.** | | Evaluate today. Review tomorrow. Send thank you notes. | Same as Monday. | Same as Monday. | Same as Monday. | Same as Monday and review the week. | |

## JOB SEARCH SCHEDULE
### Week of ________________

| Time | Sunday | Monday | Tuesday | Wednesday | Thursday | Friday | Saturday |
|------|--------|--------|---------|-----------|----------|--------|----------|
| 8:00 a.m. | | | | | | | |
| 9:00 a.m. | | | | | | | |
| 10:00 a.m. | | | | | | | |
| 11:00 a.m. | | | | | | | |
| 12:00 p.m. | | | | | | | |
| 1:00 p.m. | | | | | | | |
| 2:00 p.m. | | | | | | | |
| 3:00 p.m. | | | | | | | |
| 4:00 p.m. | | | | | | | |
| 5:00 p.m. | | | | | | | |

## JOB LEAD

*No matter where you get your job leads, it is important to keep track of them. Follow up on each lead. They may provide you with other job leads. Ask for other contacts or leads.*

| | |
|---|---|
| **Employer:** | |
| **Contact Person:** | |
| **Postal Address:** | |
| **Email Address:** | |
| **Phone/Fax:** | |
| **Company website:** | |
| **Position:** | |
| **Source of Job Lead:** | |
| **Response:** | |
| **Date Sent or Faxed Resume :** | |
| **Follow-up Date:** | |
| **Results and Other Useful Information:** | |

# NOTES

# CHAPTER 3

# Identifying Your Skills

*"Although people are accused of not knowing their own weakness, yet perhaps few know their own strength. It is in people as in soils, where sometimes there is a vein of gold which the owner knows not of."*

— JONATHAN SWIFT

Highlighting your skills in resumes, cover letters and interviews is part of the foundation of a successful job search.

Employers want to know more than your past job titles. They want to know your talents and what you have done with them. If you were to purchase a product that would cost thousands of dollars annually, you would want to know how its features could help you.

Many people have a hard time identifying their skills. Don't think of a skill as something that requires years of formal education and experience to develop. A skill is something you are doing right now in your life. In fact, job experts such as Richard Bolles suggest the average person has between 500 and 800 identifiable skills, an impressive figure, though no employer will want to hear every one of them. Instead, you need to identify at least 10 to 20 employer-attracting skills worthy of mention and bolstered by evidence of accomplishment on your resume.

There's a method to identifying, describing and promoting your skill set that we'll now investigate.

## WHAT ARE YOU GOOD AT?

One way to think about skills is to consider yourself a product and employers as consumers. What skills are going to be of use in a particular job or company? What product attributes do you bring to the table? What problem can you solve for an employer?

Think hard about your career, life and interests and then examine the lists we've created in the following pages to guide you in your skill-identifying journey.

Take a good look at yourself. Consider your personality. Good at self-management? Are you punctual, dependable, creative, independent, flexible and ambitious? Good for you. You just listed six skills.

Work in an office on a computer? That's not just one skill, it's many: typing, writing, editing and meeting deadlines. A computer programmer troubleshooting a network failure uses proofreading skills to find errors in computer codes. A cook uses slicing and cleaning skills to prepare vegetables. To complete tasks in the course of our daily lives, we balance checking accounts, manage budgets, shop and drive.

Those are skills.

Some of those skills are employed at jobs, others in life. Some can be used in resumes and during interviews. Others will be irrelevant. Blowing square bubbles and telling jokes are great party antics, but not so great for serious job interviews unless, of course, you're applying to a comedy troupe or the circus. Understanding skills improves your ability to identify them.

## Job Skills

Job skills are specific to a job or occupation. An administrative assistant is skilled in typing, word processing, filing, answering telephones and drafting correspondence. An accountant's skills include calculating accounts receivable and accounts payable, preparing taxes and using computer accounting programs. A marketer's skills revolve around working with creative teams, developing plans for product rollouts, presenting work in front of clients, working with various vendors and meeting deadlines.

Behind most skills lies a body of knowledge. A graphic designer knows how to create documents using Adobe's InDesign from files created in Microsoft Word. A cook knows about cooking techniques such as basting or baking. An auto mechanic is trained to fix problems in cars from eight or 10 manufacturers or more.

## TRANSFORMING EVERYDAY ACTIVITIES INTO SKILLS

Here are a few examples of home-based activities and other occupations that can fit a skill resume.

**Shopping:** Planning/organizational skills, budgeting, time management, product evaluation and nutrition.

**Yard Work/Lawn Care:** Physical endurance/coordination, equipment maintenance, safety operations, chemical applications, goal setting.

**Administrative Assistant**: Typing, word processing, tactfulness, timeliness, responsible, creative, dependable, detail-oriented, sincere, meeting deadlines, communicating, helping others, problem solving, checking for accuracy, researching, writing clearly and concisely.

**Answering Telephones:** Listening, mediating, communicating, respectful, helpful, resolving conflict, developing rapport, assertiveness, dependable, outgoing, pleasant, sensitive, tolerant, detail-oriented, enthusiastic, friendly, intelligent, kind, mature, patient, sincere, tactful, understanding.

Job skills do not always come from employment. They may be developed through education, hobbies, community activities and life experiences. Common activities such as shopping, managing finances, leading a committee at a school, volunteering or teaching are activities that involve potential job skills.

Job skills are important to employers because they are often looking for individuals with specific talents. They may want someone who is a team player, learns fast, handles little structure, loves challenges, enjoys pursuing goals and has an agreeable personality. They may also want that same individual to have specific skills, such as working with particular software programs or the ability to drive a certain class of vehicle or operate a piece of machinery. Mix those skills together for the right employer and you will find yourself employed.

## Transferable Skills

Many talents can be applied to a variety of activities. They can transfer from one activity to another. Self-management ability and job-specific skills are transferable. If you can operate a drill press, you have skills to operate other types of machinery. If you can balance a personal bank account, you have the math aptitude to balance a business account. If you coordinate events, lead meetings, participate on teams or get involved in community activities, you have several leadership competencies that could transfer to a job.

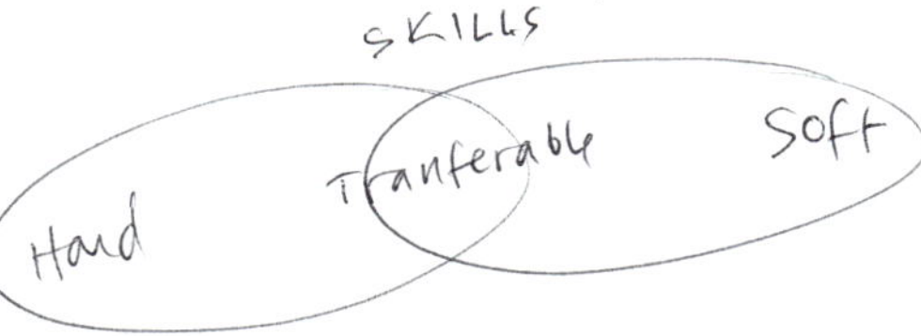

## CASE STUDY

### RESTAURANT MANAGER

**A culinary manager for 20 years,** Stan was laid off and looking for a job. Working with an employment counselor specialist in Marshall, Minn., Stan identified a host of transferable skills: time management, budgeting, employee relations, negotiating and scheduling. He managed banquets as large as 500 people and understood supply chain management and logistics.

Restaurants, of course, are customer-service oriented — at least the successful ones — and require employees to have good communication skills and a touch of human relations management. Stan had covered all that ground, and much more, in his time in the industry.

Stan put together a resume strong on transferable skills, and they put it on a well-known job board, where someone at an automotive service center chain saw it. The chain's vice president called Stan to ask him to come in for an interview and heard this response: "My only experience with grease and oil is cooking it."

In the end, Stan wasn't interested in the job. He wound up back in the food and service industry and eventually landed a managerial position he loves. The initial skepticism about transferable skills has evaporated, and he now looks for them in applicants who might not have much in the way of a food service background but do have the necessary abilities to potentially succeed, as he did, in the field.

In essence, transferable skills are proficiencies developed in a profession, previous employment or volunteer or hobby activities. For job seekers who want to try a different career, transferable skills will be a big deal on their resumes because their work histories alone might not convince employers they can flourish in a new environment. The transferable skills they delineate on their resumes will have to offer a compelling argument for their consideration.

That makes transferable skills all the more important for many reasons. Many job seekers are unlikely to find a job identical to their previous employment. Therefore, carefully evaluating how your skills transfer into other opportunities is critical. People seeking their first job, making a major career change or returning to employment after a long absence will mostly use transferable skills in their job search.

## Self-Management Skills

These are skills you use day-to-day to get along with others. They are the skills that make you unique. Examples of self-management skills are sincerity, reliability, tactfulness, patience, flexibility, timeliness and tolerance. Alongside those skills are motivation, persistence, drive and cooperation.

Do not underestimate self-management skills, especially if they show motivation and a good work attitude. These abilities are especially important for people who are seeking their first job or returning to employment after an absence.

## Emotional Intelligence

Are you able to manage your own emotions and instinctively understand or detect those of colleagues, friends and acquaintances? You may be blessed with emotional intelligence, another discipline in the evolving skills toolset that has gained traction ever since Daniel Goleman put the term on the map in his bestselling 1995 book "Emotional Intelligence: Why It Can Matter More Than IQ."

Defining it isn't all that easy. Peter Salovey and John Mayer, two leading experts on emotional intelligence who have authored several books on the topic, put it this way: "We define emotional intelligence as the subset of social intelligence that involves the ability to monitor one's own and others' feelings and emotions, to discriminate among them and to use this information to guide one's thinking and actions."

Emotional intelligence isn't just essential in the workplace. It's also an important trait to possess during the job hunt, especially when setbacks occur. Being able to find the energy to send out one more resume, make one more call, hit that networking meeting another time speaks not only to persistence but to the ability to manage your own emotions and not be defeated by them. Job hunting can be incredibly difficult, and staying positive and engaged in the process can be daunting. Yet it is the key to your success. And it requires emotional intelligence.

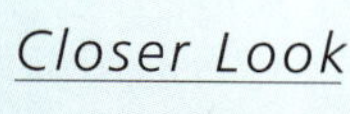

*Closer Look*

## GETTING A GRIP ON EMOTIONAL INTELLIGENCE

On a more global scale, one Twin Cities company that has embraced emotional intelligence is Ameriprise Financial. Ameriprise employs thousands of financial planners who have to deal with a roller coaster of emotions, from dealing with people who may speak to them several times before turning down their services to delivering bad news to clients about slow markets and declining stock markets.

Advocates of emotional intelligence believe you can train your brain to deal with the stress of disappointment and to nurture resilience. Those qualities are particularly valuable in sales positions, but they have to be maintained during your job hunt, too, since much of what you will be doing involves selling yourself, a challenge that may cause episodes of disillusionment even in the most resilient among us. Emotional intelligence means if a letter comes with a 'sorry, you didn't get the position' line, you keep networking and looking for a job.

## SKILLS VERSUS JOB TRAINING

St. Paul Pioneer Press columnist and career consultant Amy Lindgren has an interesting take on job training. She says that job training only "approximates" what employers need and that most jobs require talents well beyond what any class or certificate program offers.

"Employers hire workers to DO something, not to BE something," she writes. "That is, they need you to perform tasks, not to simply be certified whatever. Obvious, but easy to forget."

Her approach? If you need a license to do a job, get one. If being certified might help you find a job, take short-term classes and look for contract assignments or other hands-on experiences. Look for volunteer opportunities. Or take on a few do-it-yourself gigs to reveal your talents in a field.

And do not undertake a skills-building effort in the dark. Talk to employers, says Lindgren. "By identifying the organizations you'd like to work for and then speaking with managers about the skills they need, you'll be able to focus on the true goal, which is to be skilled and employable, not simply trained."

### FOUR STEPS TOWARD IDENTIFYING YOUR SKILLS

**Step 1:** Write the title of an employment-related activity. Focus on those activities that potentially demonstrate skill and experience relative to employment. You may get these titles from skills you gained while working for community organizations, volunteer activities and employers.

**Step 2:** List the tasks involved in performing this activity. Tasks are the basic functions of an activity.

**Step 3:** List the skills involved in accomplishing each task. Be sure to include job, self-management and transferable skills.

**Step 4:** Network with friends, associates and family. Ask them what skills they see that you have.

## Developing Skills While Looking for a Job

You should consider spending time developing new skills through volunteering. Don't volunteer, of course, only for that reason. Yet be mindful that community organizations need help, and you have plenty to offer while you try out new career options, experiences and, potentially, leadership roles.

Every community usually has an organization — United Way is a major one — that helps people find volunteer opportunities. In larger cities, the openings are fairly numerous in most cases. Check your community newspaper, too, because many have a weekly feature listing volunteer opportunities in your neighborhood or your city.

In the Twin Cities, the following organizations are set up to match volunteers: Volunteer Match (www.volunteermatch.org), Greater Twin Cities United Way (www.gtcuw.org) and Hands on Twin Cities (www.handsontwincities.org).

## PERSONAL BRANDING

*"The goal of personal branding is to be recruited based on your brand, not applying for jobs."*

— DAN SCHAWBEL,
PERSONAL BRANDING EXPERT FOR GEN-Y

Using the list of skills you have identified in this chapter, you can put them to work by developing what is called a "personal brand." You are not just a job seeker or a face in the crowd. Management consultant Tom Peters first suggested the concept in a 1997 article in Fast Company magazine, and ever since then a cottage industry of consultants has popped up to help job seekers personal brand, along with a host of books and magazine articles devoted to the topic.

Your skills make up a multi-faceted business that provides an essential service to your clients (employers). When a new brand is launched, the company thinks about what makes its product unique. Next, it creates a campaign to convince people that your brand is the best to fill a position.

Savvy job seekers will think of themselves in a similar way. What makes me unique? How can I convince employers I am the best candidate for this job? Personal branding is valuable to a job search because it helps you define who you are. Simply, it is the process by which individuals identify and communicate their unique skills to others.

## Developing a Personal Brand

Dan Schawbel, author of "Me 2.0: Build a Powerful Brand to Achieve Career Success," suggests a four-step process for personal branding: discover, create, communicate, maintain.

_Discover_ starts with determining what you want in a job or career.

_Create_ and _communicate_ focus on resumes, LinkedIn, online profiles, blogs, Twitter and Facebook, all potential portfolio material for your "brand tool kit." Maintain deals with monitoring how your brand is noted, an easy thing to do with Google Alert (www.google.com/alerts) and other Web-based tracking sites. You'll want to know what others are saying about you, and if it's wrong you can quickly correct those impressions.

_A few other points about personal branding_: You have to be consistent. You have to contribute to various online media to keep your name and brand fresh, whether it is through a personal blog or a Facebook contribution.

_You have to get out of the house_. While a lot of personal branding occurs online, the majority happens in real time. You have to attend networking functions, conferences and informational interviews. Press the flesh and hand out plenty of business cards with your website, blog and phone number. If you wish, list the social networking sites you use so that contacts can "friend" you or become your follower on Twitter.

In addition, if you develop a personal brand you must also accept the responsibility to keep it up. While personal branding is helpful during your job search, it needs to continue evolving even after you have won a new job. Make sure your "tools" are always honest and updated. Your personal brand will evolve as you gain new skills. But take care not to spend company time nurturing your personal brand on the job, which can be grounds for your boss showing you the door.

## A Final Note on Personal Branding

As personal branding has risen to prominence it seems many practitioners are Web-savvy self-promoters in media, marketing and technology. A word to the wise: Are others in your field personal branding? If you're looking for a job, do employers appreciate your ability to blog, to maintain a cool website, to stay abreast of social media?

If not, and if you're not going into self-employed consulting, it may be better to focus your efforts on other activities.

# ENDNOTES: Listing Attributes

The next section focuses on lists of skills you can use to describe your talents. These can be deployed on a resume, in cover letters and in conversations with various employers. Obviously, your career and personality won't fit all these attributes, and if they do you're being dishonest.

## GENERAL TRAITS

*What kind of person are you? General traits describe you, not just as an employee, but as a human being. The descriptive words offered below will give you an idea of the many positive things you can say about yourself.*

| | | | |
|---|---|---|---|
| Able | Ethical | Logical | Rational |
| Accepting | Extroverted | Loving | Realistic |
| Active | Fair | Mature | Reasonable |
| Adaptable | Frank | Modest | Reassuring |
| Ambitious | Friendly | Observant | Reflective |
| Assertive | Thrifty | Organized | Relaxed |
| Bold | Gentle | Original | Reliable |
| Bright | Giving | Passive | Reserved |
| Calm | Helpful | Patient | Resolute |
| Caring | Honorable | Perceptive | Respectful |
| Certain | Idealistic | Perfectionist | Responsible |
| Cheerful | Imaginative | Persuasive | Responsive |
| Clever | Independent | Playful | Satisfied |
| Confident | Innovative | Pleasant | Scientific |
| Courageous | Intelligent | Poised | Searching |
| Creative | Introverted | Powerful | Sensitive |
| Dependable | Intuitive | Precise | Spiritual |
| Determined | Jovial | Principled | Useful |
| Dignified | Kind | Progressive | Warm |
| Disciplined | Knowledgeable | Protective | Wise |
| Dutiful | Liberal | Questioning | Witty |
| Efficient | Lively | Quiet | Youthful |

## JOB SKILLS

*The following is a short list of job skills. There are thousands of job-specific skills.*
*You will have to research the job skills specific to your occupation.*

| | | |
|---|---|---|
| Accounting | Drill Press Operation | Scheduling |
| Auditing | Driving | Soldering |
| Brake Alignments | Editing | Teaching |
| Building Maintenance | Electronic Repair | Technical Writing |
| Carpet Laying | Filing | Telemarketing |
| Cleaning | Hammering | Typing |
| Computer Programming | Interviewing | Welding |
| CNC Machine Operation | Keyboarding | Writing |
| Composite Engineering | System Administration | Spreadsheet Software |
| Cooking | Management | Presentation Making Software |
| Counseling | Mechanical Drafting | Publishing Software |
| Customer Service | Metal Fabrication | Word Processing Software |
| Desktop Publishing | Payroll Accounting | Graphic Design Software |
| Detailing | Public Speaking | Web Design Software |

## SELF-MANAGEMENT SKILLS

*You use self-management skills every day to survive.*
*Self-management critical and adaptive skills are important*
*because employers hire people who will fit in with the work group.*

### CRITICAL SKILLS

| | | |
|---|---|---|
| Follow Instructions | Get Things Done | Punctual |
| Get Along Well with Others | Honest | Responsible |

### ADAPTIVE SKILLS

| | | |
|---|---|---|
| Assertive | Integrity | Self-Motivated |
| Assume Responsibility | Intelligent | Sense of Direction (Purpose) |
| Competitive | Inventive | Sense of Humor |
| Complete Assignments | Kind | Sensitive |
| Creative | Learn Quickly | Sincere |
| Decisive | Mature | Sociable |
| Dependable | Open-Minded | Tactful |
| Detail-Oriented | Outgoing | Tolerant |
| Diplomatic | Patient | Tough |
| Enthusiastic | Persistent | Trusting |
| Flexible | Physically Strong | Understanding |
| Friendly | Pleasant | Willing to Learn New Things |
| Highly Motivated | Proud of Doing a Good Job | |
| Ingenious | Results-Oriented | |

# TRANSFERABLE SKILLS

*Transferable skills can be transferred from one job or even one career to another.*
*Critical transferable skills may get you higher levels of responsibility and pay.*
*Emphasize them in an interview as well as on your resume.*

## CRITICAL TRANSFERABLE SKILLS

| | | |
|---|---|---|
| Accept Responsibility | Meet Deadlines | Sales |
| Budgeting | Project Planning | Supervise Others |
| Efficiency | Public Speaking | |

## MECHANICAL SKILLS

| | | |
|---|---|---|
| Assembling | Grinding | Operating Machines |
| Balancing, Juggling | Hammering | Physical Agility, Strength |
| Counting | Hand Crafts | Precise, Tolerance, Standards |
| Drawing, Painting | Keyboarding, Typing | Restoring |
| Driving | Keypunching, Drilling | Sandblasting |
| Endurance | Manual Dexterity | Sewing |
| Finishing, Refinishing | Modeling, Remodeling | Sorting |
| Gathering | Observing, Inspecting | Weaving |

## PEOPLE SKILLS

| | | |
|---|---|---|
| Caring | Empathy | Mentoring |
| Comforting | Encouraging | Motivating |
| Communicating | Group Facilitating | Negotiating |
| Conflict Management | Helping Others | Outgoing |
| Conflict Resolution | Inspiring Trust | Problem Solving |
| Counseling | Inquiry | Respect |
| Consulting | Instructing | Responsive |
| Developing Rapport | Interviewing | Sensitive |
| Diplomacy | Listening | Sympathy |
| Diversity | Mediating | Tolerance |

## TRANSFERABLE SKILLS (CONTINUED)

### DEALING WITH DATA

| | | |
|---|---|---|
| Analyzing | Cost Analysis | Investigating |
| Auditing | Counting | Interrelate |
| Averaging | Detail-Oriented | Organizing |
| Budgeting | Evaluating | Problem Solving |
| Calculating, Computing | Examining | Recording Facts |
| Checking for Accuracy | Financial or Fiscal Analysis | Research |
| Classifying | Financial Management | Surveying |
| Comparing | Financial Records | Synthesizing |
| Compiling | Following Instructions | Taking Inventory |

### USING WORDS AND IDEAS

| | | |
|---|---|---|
| Advertising | Imaginative | Quick Thinking |
| Articulate | Inventive | Sign Language |
| Brainstorming | Logical | Speech Writing |
| Correspondence | Promotional Writing | Telephone Skills |
| Design | Public Speaking | Write Clearly, Concisely |
| Edit | Publicity | Verbal Communication |

### LEADERSHIP

| | | |
|---|---|---|
| Competitive | Integrity | Risk Taker |
| Coordinating | Judgment | Run Meetings |
| Decision Making | Manage, Direct Others | Self-Confident |
| Decisive | Mediate Problems | Self-Directed |
| Delegate | Motivate People | Self-Motivated |
| Direct Others | Multitasking | Sets an Example, Sets Pace |
| Evaluation | Negotiate Agreements | Solve Problems |
| Goal Setting | Organization | Strategic Planning |
| Influence Others | Planning | Supervision |
| Initiate New Tasks | Results-Oriented | Work Schedules |

## TRANSFERABLE SKILLS (CONTINUED)

### —— CREATIVE ——

| | | |
|---|---|---|
| Artistic | Illustrating, Sketching | Poetic Images |
| Dance, Body Movement | Mechanical Drawing | Present Artistic Ideas |
| Designing | Model-Making | Rendering |
| Drawing, Painting | Perform | Singing |
| Expressive | Photography | Visualize Shapes |
| Handicrafts | Playing a Musical Instrument | Visualizing |

## OCCUPATIONAL TITLES

*Use the following list of job titles as a brainstorming tool when considering job goals.*

| | | |
|---|---|---|
| Accountant | Dentist | Machinist |
| Administrative Assistant | Doctor | Manager |
| Architect | Drafter | Mason |
| Assembler | Editor | Nurse |
| Cabinet Maker | Engineer | Painter |
| Carpenter | Financial Analyst | Programmer |
| Cashier | Graphic Designer | Salesperson |
| Chef | Inspector | Scientist |
| Clerk | Lab Technician | Teacher |
| Cook | Librarian | Veterinarian |
| Counselor | Machine Operator | Welder |

For a more complete list of occupational titles, visit O*Net, www.onetonline.org/,
or iseek, www.iseek.org/ .

## EMPLOYMENT-RELATED TITLES

*Community involvement and volunteer experience may be a valuable resource for your job search.*
*Describing your volunteer roles is sometimes challenging, but here's an example of common titles.*
*Just attach the name of the activity or community organization.*

*Example — YMCA Volunteer or School Fundraiser*

| | | | |
|---|---|---|---|
| Campaigner | Fundraiser | Promoter | Teacher |
| Consultant | Leader | Secretary | Treasurer |
| Coordinator | Member | Solicitor | Volunteer |
| Director | Organizer | Sponsor | Worker |

## JOB SKILLS IDENTIFICATION

*Describe four major tasks you have performed in previous employment*
*that you would like to continue using in your next job.*
*List the skills that were required to perform each task well.*

**Job Title:**

| Task ______________________ | Skills ______________________ |
|---|---|
| Task ______________________ | Skills ______________________ |
| Task ______________________ | Skills ______________________ |
| Task ______________________ | Skills ______________________ |

# CHAPTER 4

# Tools of the Job-Hunting Trade

## Resumes, Cover Letters and Business Cards

*"Emphasize your strengths on your resume, in your cover letters and in your interviews. It may sound obvious, but you'd be surprised how many people simply list everything they've ever done. Convey your passion and link your strengths to measurable results. Employers and interviewers love concrete data."*

— MARCUS BUCKINGHAM, BEST-SELLING AUTHOR AND MOTIVATIONAL SPEAKER

Before attending a networking group, cold calling a company or applying for a job, you should have a toolkit of marketing materials that tell people who you are and describe your skills and career. In a time of overwhelmed employers and loads of competition your job search toolkit — resumes, cover letters, business cards for networking, and online or hard copy portfolios — need to capture the attention of employers.

The resume, of course, is a key element of any job search. It will not get you the job, but it may get you in the door. It recaps your personal and professional skills and highlights your career accomplishments. Many, but not all job applications will require you to submit a cover letter with your resume. In this chapter, we'll show you how to write a resume and cover letter that will match your qualifications and experience to a specific job opening. We'll give you tips on how to submit your cover letter and resume in digital formats plus share resume and cover letter templates that have been effective for others.

The business card is a necessity of networking. Not everyone will want a copy of your resume when you meet them, especially if it's at a professional networking mixer, a social function or even a party at your brother-in-law's home. That's where the business card comes in.

Providing a portfolio is common for people in advertising, public relations, marketing, journalism, sales and the arts. Portfolios, of course, are adaptable to almost all professions and work well for college students entering the workforce or people returning to the workforce. Just like a resume, a portfolio can take many forms. All portfolios, especially online versions such as your own Pinterest board, offer you a richer palette of possibilities for visually describing your life and career. It's a nice addition to a standard resume and gives you a chance to stretch your creativity.

# RESUMES

Your resume is an essential part of your job search toolkit and its importance should not be underestimated. You will need one for whatever kind of job you are looking for. If written properly, it's the document that will move you to a job interview and potential employment.

Do not approach the task of writing the resume lightly. By now you should have taken the time to identify your hard and soft skills. If you cannot identify at least 20 job-related skills at this point, your first task is to revisit Chapter 3 on skills and create your list.

Be aware that your resume is never really done. You have to customize it to match the qualifications and skills sought by employers for specific jobs.

Job seekers start out at different points when preparing resumes. Some will have a resume a few months or a few years old. Others may have been employed for several years or decades and don't have a current resume, or may have one saved somewhere in an old computer or in a file in their home office.

## Four Steps to Get Started

Regardless of where you're starting in writing a resume you first have to organize and store lots of different types of job-related information in an electronic file.

**1.** **Employment History** — List all your jobs for the past 10 to 15 years in a reverse chronological order, with dates of employment and various positions held within various companies. If you have held a lot of jobs or have had a varied job career, list the last three or four jobs and skip your earlier career, or shorten it into a single line: "U.S. Bank, Minneapolis, MN, teller, 2005-2010."

**2.** **Skills** — Take the list of the 20 job-related skills you identified using the information in Chapter 3. Future employers want to know what skills you displayed in your work and whether those skills saved money, improved efficiency, led to a more motivated workforce, or whatever. Ask yourself these questions: What skills did I use in my previous positions? Are they important to the employers or jobs that I am considering?

**3.** **Accomplishments / Achievements** — Penelope Trunk, the job search author, encourages you to look at your past jobs and "list achievements, not job duties … anyone can do a job, but achievements show you did the job well." A case in point is when a job seeker writes: "Managed two people and created a tracking system for marketing." Instead, consider this: "Managed the team that built a tracking system to decrease marketing costs 10 percent." The second example obviously sounds more impressive.

Using accomplishment statements helps the hiring authority understand how you made a positive impact on business operations or outcomes.

Mark Zappa, who works in the Minnesota WorkForce Center in North St. Paul, Minn., points out that an accomplishment can be an actual testimonial from a supervisor — a nice break from the usual standard resume information. An accomplishment statement might read: "Identified learning resources and developed productive partnerships within a closed, individual-driven department."

**4.** **Job Search Goals** — Establish clear objectives for your search. What kind of company do you want to work for? What size? In what field? What sorts of jobs are you seeking?

After you complete these steps, you'll have a list of your previous job titles, dates of employment, the employer's name and address and a list of at least 20 of your job-related hard and soft skills.

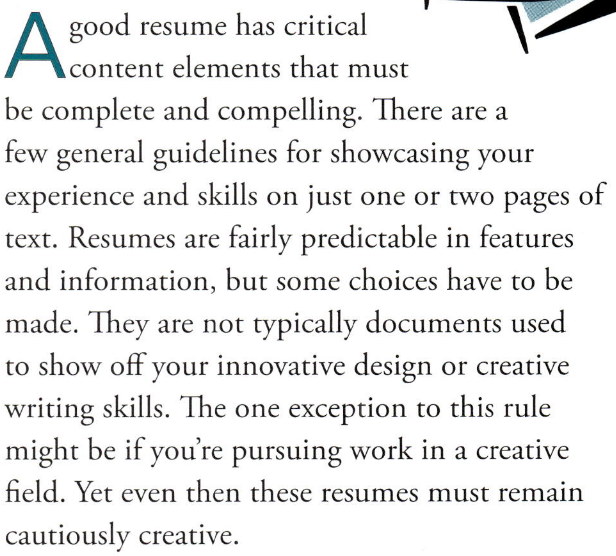


# WRITING THE RESUME

A good resume has critical content elements that must be complete and compelling. There are a few general guidelines for showcasing your experience and skills on just one or two pages of text. Resumes are fairly predictable in features and information, but some choices have to be made. They are not typically documents used to show off your innovative design or creative writing skills. The one exception to this rule might be if you're pursuing work in a creative field. Yet even then these resumes must remain cautiously creative.

Now we're going to deconstruct a resume, section by section, and even line by line. We'll start at the top, end at the bottom. Don't worry about the final look or format of your resume just yet. Start with the core content. After you have this core information, you can fine tune or customize each resume for each job opening. This is called "targeting" your resume.

## Font Selection

There are two types of fonts, serif and sans serif. Serif fonts have tails or feet and sans serif fonts do not. Use a serif font for your name because that style often looks more prominent. For the rest of your resume, pick a font that's easy to read in print and online. Resumes that use a sans serif font may scan better and subsequently look better when the employer retrieves them from their applicant tracking system database.

### Serif Fonts

Baskerville Old
Bell MT
**Bodoni**
Bookman Antiqua
Century
**Garamond**
Georgia
Goudy Old Style
Times New Roman

### Sans Serif Fonts

Arial
Helvetica
Century Gothic
Charlotte Sans
Candara
Gill Sans
Lucida Sans
Myriad
Verdana

## Name Block

Put your full first and last names on its own line at the top of the page. Choose your favorite professional-looking font. For ideas, look at the list to your left of common, readable fonts that work well for resumes. Your name can be in a different font than the body of the resume. Type your name in bold or CAPITAL LETTERS to make it stand out, and make it larger point type than the body of the resume.

Your address should not contain abbreviations. Include all 10 digits of your landline phone or mobile number. It should be a number where you can be reached at all times. Use a professional personal email address. Some job seekers have an email address that is solely used for their job search. If applicable, also include your LinkedIn profile address. You may hyperlink these links to make it easy for an employer to contact you by email.

**Elizabeth Applicant**

1443 HireMe Lane
Employmentville, Minnesota 55555

555-555-5555

Elizabeth.Applicant@fakemail.com

## Objective   *Headline - compelling*

Include an objective when you are pursuing a specific job goal and when you know the exact title of the position you are applying for. The objective statement helps target your resume. When applying for a specific job, use the title in your objective and even add the name of the company as in the following example:

"Objective: Landscape Design Specialist at Creative Environments Inc." Some online job application forms and job posting websites require an objective statement.

Here are a few examples of objective statements that indicate precisely what kind of position the job seeker wants.

- Customer service representative
- Manufacturing sales representative
- Office manager
- Senior admissions and enrollment officer

## Summary Section

Your resume should include an effective Summary Section that briefly highlights your recent work experience (including industries you've worked in), applicable certifications, achievements and skills that best match the position for which you are applying. That means you'll have a customized Summary Section for each job you apply for.

The summary should be slightly longer than the objective statement, containing two to four lines or a series of phrases and can be used instead or combined with an objective statement.

Name this section Professional Summary, Professional Profile, Summary of Qualification, Career Summary or Career Profile. Below are two examples:

## Objective: Landscape Architect

Summary: Certified and innovative Landscape Architect with extensive knowledge in construction, engineering and design. Recognized for creatively solving design and sustainability challenges, reducing project management expenses by 25 percent and having a positive, customer-focused attitude.

## Professional Profile

Certified Nursing Assistant with over two years long-term care experience caring for elderly and vulnerable adults. Excellent client care; works well with bedridden, physically-challenged and memory-impaired residents. Commended for superior safety and attendance record. Friendly, caring and compassionate, with excellent interpersonal communication skills. Flexible: available days, evenings, weekends and holidays. Maintains confidential information.

## Skills Section

Include a skills section to quickly and effectively communicate your experience and make yourself stand out from other applicants. Match your skills (used in volunteer and paid positions) from the list you have already created with the requirements and preferences included in the job posting. Formats for skill lists include:

### 1. Bullet Point List with Results

Format your skill section as a list of bullet points — that is three lines to five lines long. Limit each entry to two lines. Choose action verbs that demonstrate responsibility. For example, "managed," "coordinated" or "designed." Vary the action verbs that you choose. This helps make your abilities sound more diverse and adds depth to your resume. Use the list of action verbs provided in this chapter and in the job opening itself for ideas. Review your list of accomplishment statements to quantify your results.

### 2. Grouping Skills by Topic

Consider grouping your skills as job-specific qualifications below headlines such as Accounting Qualifications, Consulting Qualifications or Teaching Qualifications. Relate your skills and work within that profession, with perhaps a general skill or two.

### 3. Skill List

This format is often used to list your competency using computers. Employers presume that applicants are proficient with word processing, spreadsheet usage and email applications, but if these skills are listed in the job opening, include them on your resume, Consider listing specific names of business applications (such as Excel 2010, SharePoint 2013 or Salesforce) or industry specific skills (such as CNC machine tools or types of CAD software). Use a bulleted list, three to five lines long.

Use the table below to create a Skill List to apply for jobs with an employer's applicant tracking system. Mirror the words used in the employer's job posting to receive yet another opportunity for the software to match your resume to the job opening and for you to be found in a keyword search of job applicants.

**THINK CREATIVELY.**
**CONSIDER THESE EXAMPLES OF STRONG SKILLS STATEMENTS:**

| | |
|---|---|
| **Before:** Answered phones | **After:** Responded to an average of 200 service inquiry phone calls per day in a helpful and professional manner. |
| **Before:** Waited tables | **After:** Managed and maintained eight tables, utilizing interpersonal skills to ensure customer satisfaction through prompt, cordial service. |
| **Before:** Drove a truck | **After:** Responsible for ensuring safe and efficient delivery of goods to over 15 vendors while driving a highly sophisticated vehicle. |

*This information was provided by the University of Minnesota Career and Community Learning Center.*

## Employment History

List your most recent employment first. A general standard is to chronologically list in reverse order the last three to four jobs or those you have had over the past 10 years. Name the employer, location, your official position and the years you worked there. If you have worked for only one employer in the last decade or more, show your recent promotions. If your job title did not change in the last decade you can still show job progression by showcasing how you took on more complex job tasks and increased responsibilities.

How much information should you give about your past jobs? Focus on what you did and your accomplishments in various positions. Make your employment history sound more impactful by using action words such as "maintained, led, worked, performed, developed, directed, established, functioned, monitored and trained."

Use bullet points and make your sentences one line. Sentence fragments like "specialized in training employees to use proprietary software that resulted in a 15 percent reduction in data entry errors" work fine. List no more than four to six bullet points in describing your last job. Then use two to three points for subsequent positions.

Although contact information is typically given on an application or reference sheet, many resumes still list the employer name, city and state. Other job seekers might limit this information to keep the resume focused on skills, accomplishments and qualifications that best match the job opening. The choice is yours. There is no single standard that fits all situations.

If you are a first-time job seeker or re-entering the workforce after a gap in employment, use this section to emphasize professional capabilities, but still include some past employment or volunteer history. Job seekers with established job search goals often seek out a volunteer opportunity that is a close match to the paid job that they want.

## Education

If more of your skills and experience come from employment, list employment first and education last. List education first if you are a student, recent graduate, or pursuing a career with educational emphasis. Include the name of the institution, location (city and state), graduation date or projected graduation date, degree(s) earned, field of study and GPA (if over 3.0).

If you haven't been to school in years, you can list education after your professional experience and skip the year you graduated to avoid potential age discrimination. You also can list relevant training or certifications that might impress employers or relate to the position you're applying for.

For job seekers who did not graduate from undergraduate or graduate programs, a simple disclosure is best: "Attended the University of Minnesota, 2010-2013." It shows you have ambition even though you didn't graduate.

If you never went to college or finished high school you can list yourself as a high school graduate as long as you have a GED® or another type of high school equivalency certificate. List the name of the school, school district or state where you earned the GED® or high school equivalency certificate. Do not include an education section if you did not finish high school and had no formal training either in school or from an employer.

Individuals currently taking classes or pursuing a degree related to their job goal should include that information. List the skills acquired, academic accomplishments and the projected date of completion.

## Memberships

List organizational memberships related to your job goal. Avoid using non-employer-related or controversial organizations. Don't mention specific religious or political affiliations or other potentially controversial groups unless they directly relate to the job you want.

## Military Experience

Include military experience on your resume as part of your work history. If you are targeting a job within the defense industry, feel free to use military jargon. The defense industry likes candidates who understand the lingo. If you are targeting a job outside of the defense arena, you will need to "civilianize" your military language to show that your skills and experience match the employer's needs. See Resources Section (page 70) for a list of military to civilian job skills.

## Volunteer Experience

Volunteer experience can fill in any gaps in employment. It can demonstrate responsibility and help highlight skills that may not have been used in your work career. Served as an officer of the PTA? Or a coach at your children's school? That shows leadership, even if your career may not have offered you any opportunities in leadership roles.

## Hobbies/Personal Interests

Include hobbies and personal interests if they're employment-related, not controversial, and show skills and experience.

## References

Do not include your references or the phrase "references available on request" on the actual resume. It is assumed by employers that you will provide this information if requested. Once an employer asks for your references, provide the names and contact information of three to five people who can speak favorably about your attributes.

## Awards/Recognition

Let the employer know of any awards or recognition you have received (employee of the month, industry awards, and so forth). Those are accomplishments worthy of mention.

## TARGETING YOUR RESUME

Targeted resumes are a necessity for most job openings. Why? Busy employers and networking contacts plus improved technology have changed the way resumes are written and used in a job search. Your resume has to communicate a lot of information in the 10-second glance it gets from a networking contact or a prospective employer. If the employer uses an applicant tracking system (ATS) it first has to successfully pass electronic screening and resume ranking before it is read by the hiring authority. Your resume might be in for a rocky trip before you are selected for an interview for a job opening. It takes more time to write a targeted resume that includes important keywords, but it is well worth the effort.

Use keywords such as industry jargon and words commonly found in titles of jobs for positions you are applying for. The keywords in your targeted resume will help you stand out in an ATS because it's set up to identify specific skills of applicants. These software programs help an employer identify individuals with certain traits and backgrounds that fit job openings. Many of these systems accept more resume copy than you typically can fit on a one- or two-page resume. Use this opportunity to include more of your relevant experience and skills. Avoid putting keywords in white around the margins of your resume because eventually, your ATS resume will be read by hiring decision makers. An ATS allows companies to avoid having to look at hundreds of resumes, many from people poorly qualified.

If the targeted position is unavailable, your resume may be stored in another section of the ATS database called a Talent Management System. Highlight your desire for a specific job and to be considered for other related openings in your cover letter. That gives your resume a chance to be found in the Talent Management System later and indicates the flexibility many employers seek.

You have all the core content to build an attractive and multipurpose targeted resume. Use any one of a number of resume templates to create a visually pleasing and easy to read resume document. After you have completed the resume, you will have the flexibility to distribute your resume in plain text, save it as a PDF, send it as an email attachment, cut and paste sections of it for online job applications, or print it for networking meetings, postal-mail job applications or an interview.

## Networking Resume

Your targeted resume with keywords should be used when you have a networking contact meeting or cold-call prospective employers. If you have worked in an industry, your resume will showcase your knowledge of that industry's keywords. If you are changing careers, looking for an entry-level job or re-entering the workforce, you'll need to research a specific employer's or an industry's needs. Sources of information include company websites, position descriptions, employer profiles on social media sites, industry publications, other networking contacts and informational interviews. Use this information to adjust your skills

and experience content to fall within the needs of the employer or industry.

Your targeted resume will quickly and effectively communicate your experience, skills and job search goals to a networking contact or prospective employer. Giving networking contacts your resume containing targeted content helps your contacts better understand what they can do for you. These contacts are pipelines to what is called a "warm referral" — that personal connection to another contact or an employer who has a job opening. Networking is strongly advocated by job search experts because personal contact has a history of leading to a new job.

## Job Application Resume Format

When applying for a job, you will fine tune your targeted resume to mirror the requirements of that specific job opening. Your content must include not only your relevant experience and skills that the employer wants, but the keywords used in the job opening announcement. Your job is to show that your qualifications and experience match what the employer is seeking because employers look for resumes where the applicant has all (or nearly all) of the qualifications and experience that are in the job posting.

Start by carefully reading the job posting. Job postings tend to follow a pattern. Employers usually summarize the job responsibilities followed by the required and preferred qualifications for all applicants. Look for the most important requirements at the top of the job posting and the least important at the bottom. Targeted resumes that use the same words that the employer used to summarize the job responsibilities, qualifications and skills have a better chance of moving forward through an ATS or a manual candidate screening process.

# BASIC RESUME WRITING

When writing resumes, there are a few things to keep in mind and a few things to avoid. Resumes are a tool to get you an interview with employers by recounting your career and skills in the most economical way possible. Here's a guide for how to craft a strong resume.

**Keep It Brief:** One to two pages is just about right, unless you are a professor or a doctor. If your resume extends beyond one page, make sure that you fill at least half or more of the second page. If you cannot do this edit your resume to one page.

**Targeting:** Target your job search and your resume to your specific occupational goals. Target resumes to the level of employment, occupation or employer. Make changes to your baseline resume when you're pursuing a different occupation or you're going for a position less advanced than your former job. (This pertains in particular to workers applying for jobs that might pay less than they earned in the past.) Consider taking out information not pertinent to the job you're applying for and add in anything that illustrates the skills that the position requires.

**Provide a Visual Impact:** A resume has 10 seconds to convince hiring managers and employers that you should be interviewed, so make it readable. Use white space and bullets. Use indentation.

**Check Your Grammar and Spelling:** Double and triple check for typographical, grammatical and spelling errors and ask for another person to proofread it.

**Ensure Integrity:** Accentuate the positive, skip the negative, be honest.

**Make It Scannable and ATS Friendly:** Create a resume in RTF or DOC (Microsoft Word) format and most employers will be able to scan it. Some scanners and ATS cannot read PDF files so keep it simple.

**Print Using Quality Paper:** Use 24-pound or higher grade, 100 percent cotton fiber paper for a clear, sharp image. White, cream or gray works fine. Avoid colored paper or glossy, high shine finishes. Paper size should be the standard letter size, 8½" x 11".

**Make Clear Reproductions:** When making copies for distribution, use a laser printer when possible. Public libraries and WorkForce Centers have printers available. Office supply and copy shops may also be able to print directly from your USB drive on to your resume paper. Test a copy before making dozens of them, and collate correctly.

**Get Access to a Computer:** Having a computer and Internet connection at home is extremely beneficial to your job search. If a personal computer does not fit your budget, buy a USB drive and save your resume on it. Whenever you have access to a computer, you can work on your resume by plugging the drive into a USB port. Otherwise, there are several places to get computer access for free. Computers are available at Minnesota WorkForce Centers, friends and family, schools, social organizations, community agencies, print shops, religious organizations, county human service offices, community action agencies and public libraries.

# MAKING THE MOST OF YOUR RESUME

Resumes should be sent to a specific person. Use their name. Avoid sending the resume to a job title such as "Production Manager." It will take extra effort, but do your research and find out the name and title of the appropriate person to whom your resume should be sent.

If asked, send your resume to human resources. Then also send a resume to the person in charge of the department in which you want to work. Most of the time, human resources do the screening, but it's the department manager who is the final hiring authority.

## GENERAL RESUME TIPS

- Lead with your strongest statements that are related to the job or goal.
- Emphasize your skills.
- Keep it brief (one to two pages).
- Use 8½" x 11" paper.
- Correct all typographical, grammatical and spelling errors.
- Include your employment-related accomplishments.
- Target your qualifications.
- Clearly communicate your purpose and value to employers.
- Use the best format to showcase your skills.
- Make your resume relevant to the job.
- Always include a cover letter when mailing your resume.

## THINGS TO AVOID

- Using abbreviations (exceptions include middle initial and directions such as "N" for North).
- Using personal pronouns such as "I" to refer to you.
- Mentioning wage history.
- Using fancy typeset, binders or exotic paper.
- Sending a photograph of yourself unless it's relevant (i.e. acting, etc.).
- Making statements that you cannot prove.
- Including personal information (age, height, weight, family status, picture).
- Highlighting religious or political affiliations unless you're applying for a job with one of these organizations.
- Changing the tense of verbs or using the passive voice.
- Using the title "resume."
- Including references on the resume. (Make a separate reference sheet.)
- Including hobbies or social interests unless they contribute to your objective.
- Stapling or folding your resume.
- Using the same action word more than twice.

When mailing your resume, always send it with a cover letter. Mass-mailing your resume to employers does not work. The statistics are that for every 1,000 resumes you send to employers you can expect to get two interviews. Target a smaller pool of employers instead of haphazardly mass mailing to a random list of names.

Follow up your resume submissions with a phone call to the employer. Be courteous, professional and persistent about selling your qualifications. Be sure to ask for an interview.

When directly contacting employers, always have a copy of your resume available and take the initiative to offer it to them. Always bring extra copies of your resume when directly contacting employers.

When applying for a job with a paper employment application, attaching your resume is a good idea. The resume will add impact and should complement the application. If you're asked to fill out an application, never write on it "See resume." Filling out the entire application is still required.

Give a copy of your resume to your references. It provides them with information about you and will help them to talk to an employer about your qualifications.

Hand or send emailed copies of your resume to all networking contacts. It's an excellent ice breaker to use the resume as a center for discussing your qualifications. Ask your contacts to critique your resume.

## RESUME STRATEGIES

Once it's done, a resume is like a product. If it sits on a shelf no one will buy it. You have to promote yourself with your resume at networking events, by speaking to potential employers and by submitting it with job applications. Pass it out to the following people:

- Employers with advertised job openings
- Employers with no advertised job openings
- Employment agencies
- Vocational and college placement offices
- Personal and professional networking contacts
- Your references
- Executive recruiters
- Your employment counselors or instructors
- General and niche-based job boards

Finally, follow-up, follow-up, follow-up. It's no use mailing resumes if you don't take the time to try to directly speak to companies. The true test of an effective resume is that you're offered interviews. If you aren't getting responses or interviews from your resume, you may want to re-evaluate it.

# COVER LETTERS

Most resumes are accompanied by a cover letter or cover email. Written in business style, cover letters and cover emails should contain an expression of your interest in working for a company, an abbreviated introduction to your career and a short, compelling paragraph detailing why you would be a perfect fit for a current or future opening. Cover letters must follow the application directions that the employer stated in the job posting.

Cover letters, like resumes must be targeted for each position you seek or contact you make. Deciding what to put in the letter remains tricky since you do not want to repeat your entire resume, yet you will want to make a strong case for a company to, in fact, look at your skills and experience to see if they fit any open positions.

Cover letters and emails are employed in a variety of circumstances, ranging from applying for advertised jobs to serving as a "letter of introduction" to companies where you want to work, requesting networking leads or informational interviews. The targeted audience may be different, but the general approach remains the same.

## Cover Letter Audiences

Cover letters serve different readers. Typically, cover letters are targeted at specific job openings in a company. These "application" letters match your qualifications to a position's advertised requirements.

Another variation, the "prospecting" letter, is used to contact employers who haven't advertised or published job openings. You may have cold-called a company and gotten the name of someone you want to contact with a letter, resume and follow-up call. These letters call for describing your skills and matching them to the perceived needs of the employer based on your research.

The "networking" letter, in contrast, first refers to the person who gave you the referral before asking for an informational interview or, in the case of an opening, consideration for the position. It's fine to ask in a networking letter for recipients to share more contacts at other companies if they're willing.

Whenever you use any of these letters remember to include a second attachment — your resume.

## Tips for Writing Strong Cover Letters

*Printed Cover Letters*: Use a standard business letter format. Below your name and address — or masthead — will be the date, followed by an empty line, then the recipient's name and title, street address, city, state and ZIP code.

_**Email Cover Letters**_: Subject line — use the exact job title and any position reference numbers that are often included in job openings followed by a dash and your first and last name. Make sure that your document name matches the name you put in the subject line. Sign your email with a professional closing.

_**Address a Person**_: Always address the letter to a specific person by name and title. Even if responding to a job that states "no phone calls" consider calling to politely ask the name of the hiring authority or search through your LinkedIn network to see if one of your contacts knows the name of the hiring authority. You may not always be able to identify the name of a specific person. In this case, send the letter to the title of the recipient (Production Manager, Maintenance Supervisor, Office Manager, Human Resources or Search Committee).

_**State Your Intent**_: In general, your letter should state your interest in the job. In the case of a letter of introduction, simply state you would like to work for the company. Use the first paragraph to express your energy, enthusiasm, skills, education and work experience that could contribute to the company's success.

Use the second and third paragraphs, or a list of bullet points, that exhibit your talents, experience and achievements. These can be brief summaries of what you illuminate in greater detail in your attached resume.

_**The T Formation**_: Consider the "T" letter format, which first names the specific requirements an employer has asked for in the job posting and your corresponding qualifications. If you have collected a list of likely qualifications for the positions you seek, you can do the same thing.

The strategy might look like the following. An advertised position asks for experience managing, writing, marketing and accounting. You could in the middle section match your skill set to those abilities, as in the following example:

- _Managing_: Supervised a department of 10 employees at Marketing Inc. in Minneapolis for five years that won three national awards.

- _Writing_: Crafted more than 150 brochures and print ads, including several that won national awards.

- _Marketing_: Led a total of 12 campaigns integrating social media, print, Web, and radio for three different clients over the past three years.

- _Accounting_: Completed several financial classes toward an MBA and understand major accounting software systems.

_**The Final Paragraph**_: Use the final paragraph to mention you will make a follow-up call within a week, perhaps within a few days, to confirm the document has been received and to ask for an interview. Thank the person for taking the time to read your letter. Use a formal, professional closing.

*One More Look*: Be sure to proofread your letter to check content, grammar and spelling, and ask someone else to have a look, too. Sign printed cover letters in blue or black ink.

In writing the letters, avoid appearing too familiar, overbearing, humorous or cute. Avoid starting too many sentences or bullet points with "I" if possible. Keep sentences short and to the point. The entire letter should be one page composed of three to five paragraphs. Remember, your resume will fill in details.

*Mail First Class*: Skip business class envelopes and use 8½" x 11" mailers so you don't have to bother folding your letter and resume. A larger envelope keeps the documents flat and crisp and will be worth the extra cost.

## NETWORKING WITH BUSINESS CARDS

Creating business cards is the easiest part of any job search. If you can spell your name and write your contact information correctly, getting a business card together should be a breeze. There are a few ways to make your business card stand out from the pack. When you distribute your business cards at networking events, job fairs or conferences you will want your card to jump out yet leave a favorable impression.

Dave Taylor, an Internet veteran who has published 20 business and technical books and writes the business blog www.intuitive.com, suggests business cards must do three things: 1) supply key contact information, 2) jumpstart recipients' curiosity and 3) jog their memories. Following are some of his suggestions, as well as those of other business card experts.

- Determine the information you want on the card. Of course, you want your name, address, email and phone numbers — work, home and mobile phone. Add the URL to your LinkedIn profile, Twitter handle or Pinterest site. Some of your contacts will prefer to follow up with you through social media. If your home phone is shared by your family you might consider adding a second phone number or second line during your search.

- Check for typos. Double- and triple-check your information.

- Give a description of your profession. "Child psychologist," "Web writer and producer," "Team leader and machinist," "Financial analyst" will give the card recipient at least a small idea of your background and talent. Five or 10 words should take care of it. If you have other certifications or advanced degrees add them after your name but try not to overdo it. The downside is you may look like you're overqualified for many positions; it's a tough call as to when to highlight that information and when to keep it silent.

- Get the cards professionally printed. In a rush? Many copy shops and printers can turn around business cards in hours. Some shops even offer their services online.

- Some people use the back of the business card to list abilities. Some job experts, however, like the idea of leaving that space blank for potential employers to take notes. Like both ideas? You can compromise by listing your attributes on the back but leave room for someone to make a note or two.

- Quality matters. Use thicker card stock rather than cheaper, thinner paper. It tells potential employers you pay attention to small details, like having a business card that does not crumple or tear easily.

## Getting Creative With Business Cards

Scott Ginsberg, author of "The Power of Approachability" and writer for the online site www.businessknowhow.com, believes in getting creative with business cards. He's seen business cards of different sizes and shapes, from triangles to circles; some business commentators think 3"x5" cards at least break the mold.

He's seen cards with die-cut holes that pop up when open, that contain contact details in Braille and international languages, that carry motivational quotes or that look like baseball trading cards. One Boston banker he knows uses business cards that look like miniature checks.

He has a couple of other simple strategies to remember. Don't forget your cards before leaving home. You never know when you will run into someone who can help in your job search. If you meet a particularly well-connected individual

who seems genuinely interested in helping you land a job, give them several cards for redistribution to their contacts.

Here are a couple of other good ideas for effective business cards, among them adding a graphic, strong colors or a photo of yourself. Although black and white cards are inexpensive they will not stand out. A colored logo will help add a dash of personality.

A photo, meanwhile, connects you to recipients, reminding them of who you are when they look at their business card collection two weeks or two months after you met. One Minneapolis journalist uses a fun, colorful caricature rendered by a friend who is a cartoonist. Adding color — especially red and black — will help you stand out. A hedge fund manager in Minneapolis once used a black card with white letters simply displaying his website, which drove a remarkable amount of traffic to it from people curious for more information and from potential clients.

Do not overlook the importance of business cards. Used effectively, they are your mini-resume and have the potential to open new doors during your job search. Certainly, many recipients may toss them into a wastebasket, but hopefully they do this after they have connected to you through LinkedIn or another social media outlet. If even 10 percent keep your card you will have made a little headway in your job search.

# ENDNOTES: Action Words

The following section will be the longest of the book. It contains "action words" and many examples of resumes and cover letters. Even if you are not in the profession represented in the examples, you can certainly borrow the templates, words and techniques offered here.

## ACTION WORDS

*Use this list of action words to help you create strong skills statements.*

| | | | |
|---|---|---|---|
| Achieved | Awarded | Constructed | Directed |
| Addressed | Began | Consulted | Distributed |
| Adjusted | Budgeted | Contacted | Drafted |
| Administered | Built | Controlled | Earned |
| Advised | Calculated | Contracted | Edited |
| Advocated | Catalogued | Convinced | Effected |
| Affected | Chaired | Converted | Emphasized |
| Aided | Clarified | Coordinated | Enabled |
| Analyzed | Coached | Corrected | Encouraged |
| Applied | Collaborated | Correlated | Enforced |
| Appointed | Collected | Counseled | Engineered |
| Appraised | Communicated | Created | Enlarged |
| Approved | Compared | Customized | Enlisted |
| Arranged | Compiled | Decided | Equipped |
| Assembled | Composed | Defined | Established |
| Assessed | Conceived | Delegated | Estimated |
| Assigned | Conceptualized | Designed | Evaluated |
| Assisted | Conserved | Detailed | Examined |
| Attained | Conducted | Determined | Excelled |
| Audited | Contributed | Developed | Executed |

## ACTION WORDS *(CONTINUED)*

| | | | |
|---|---|---|---|
| Expanded | Increased | Mediated | Searched |
| Expedited | Influenced | Merged | Secured |
| Experimented | Informed | Mastered | Selected |
| Explored | Initiated | Moderated | Simplified |
| Extracted | Inspected | Modified | Sold |
| Fabricated | Inspired | Monitored | Solved |
| Facilitated | Installed | Motivated | Spoke |
| Familiarized | Instituted | Reduced | Stimulated |
| Filed | Instructed | Recorded | Streamlined |
| Focused | Integrated | Recruited | Strengthened |
| Forecasted | Interacted | Rectified | Structured |
| Formed | Interpreted | Regulated | Succeeded |
| Formulated | Interviewed | Rehabilitated | Summarized |
| Furnished | Introduced | Reinforced | Supplied |
| Furthered | Invented | Remodeled | Supported |
| Founded | Investigated | Reorganized | Tailored |
| Generated | Joined | Repaired | Taught |
| Governed | Judged | Replaced | Tested |
| Grouped | Launched | Reported | Tutored |
| Guided | Lectured | Represented | Transformed |
| Handled | Led | Researched | Translated |
| Headed | Located | Resolved | United |
| Hosted | Logged | Restored | Upgraded |
| Illustrated | Listened | Reviewed | Utilized |
| Implemented | Maintained | Revised | Validated |
| Improved | Managed | Revitalized | Verified |
| Incorporated | Marketed | Scheduled | |

## OCCUPATIONAL KEYWORDS

*Occupational keywords include skills, titles, degrees and occupational buzzwords.*

| | | | |
|---|---|---|---|
| Account Management | Cross-Cultural Training | Journeyman | Raw Materials |
| Accounts Receivable | Decision Making | Layout Design | Receptionist |
| Acquisitions | Demographics | Logic Analyzer | Reporter |
| Bachelor's Degree | Die Casting | Magnetic Theory | Research |
| Bank Reconciliation | Dietitian | Manager | Sales |
| Batch Processing | Drywall | Mapping | Secretarial |
| Benchmarking | Ecology | Marketing | Software Modeling |
| Blueprint Reading | Electronics | Master's Degree | Spanish |
| Budget | Employee Assistance | Microprocessor | Spreadsheets |
| Bulletins | Engineer | Microsoft Word | Stick Welding |
| CAD | Equipment Vendor | Microsoft Office | Strategic Planning |
| Calibrator | Facilitator | Nursing | Student Personnel |
| Carpentry | Financial Planning | Oscillator | Supervisor |
| Cash Flow | Food Preparation | Patient Advocate | Taxonomy |
| Cell Culture Media | Gas Pipeline | Payroll | Teacher |
| Cement | Goal Setting | Personal Computer | Technical Writing |
| Child Care | Graphic Design | Process Metallurgy | Time Management |
| Claims Adjudication | Guest Services | Proposal Writing | Transportation |
| Commercial Leasing | Hiring/Firing | Psychology | Travel |
| Copy Editing | Hotel | Public Relations | Wave Soldering |
| Counselor | ISO 9000 | Purchasing | Workflow |
| Crisis Management | Journalism | Radio | Writer |

# Resume Samples

The resume samples on the following pages model the basic formats and principles of resume writing. Consider how each job seeker presents his/her skills and experience. Along with the content, look at how the resume is presented. Draw the best from each to help decide how to style your resume. Ultimately, your resume will be unique to you and won't look exactly like any of these presented.

## TARGETED RESUME: Professional in Health Care

**First name Last name**
111 South Street #101, Minneapolis, Minnesota 55407
612-821-0000

### PROFESSIONAL PROFILE

**Certified Nursing Assistant** with more than two years long-term care experience caring for elderly and vulnerable adults. Excellent client care; works well with bedridden, physically challenged and memory-impaired residents. Commended for superior safety and attendance record. Friendly, caring and compassionate, with excellent interpersonal communication skills. Flexible: available days, evenings, weekends and holidays. Maintains confidential information.

### LICENSES AND CERTIFICATIONS

- Minnesota CNA License in good standing
- CPR certified

### SKILLS

- Multi-tasking
- Medical teamwork
- Bedside manner
- Infection control
- Health promotion and maintenance
- Creating a safe environment
- Good judgment in emergencies
- Pain management
- Acute / Critical care

### ACCOMPLISHMENTS

- Acknowledged for accurate completion of each resident's meal assessment and oral intake records and consistently ensuring a comfortable arrival time for their meals and activities.
- Complimented for respectful and dignified nursing care with resident's daily hygiene.
- Respected resident confidentiality and protected their privacy. Understand and follow HIPAA and protected health information (PHI) policies.
- Prevented personal and resident injury by strict adherence to procedures and proper equipment use when transferring, raising and lifting a resident.
- Followed directions of nurses and individual resident care plans.
- Recognized for completing job tasks efficiently and on time.
- Engaged residents with appropriate and personalized placement of their treasured keepsakes.

### PROFESSIONAL EXPERIENCE

*Certified Nursing Assistant,* Reliable Residential Care, St. Paul, MN        20_ _ – 20_ _
*Certified Nursing Assistant,* Care Center, That Town, MN        20_ _ – 20_ _

### EDUCATION

**Community Technical College,** Metro City, MN        December 20_ _
Nursing Assistant – Certified program

**High School Name,** That Town, MN        June 20_ _
High School Diploma – Honors Student

## TARGETED RESUME: Professional in Finance

# Susan B. Jobseeker

SBJobseeker@fakemail.com ◆ 555-555-5555 ◆ City, State, ZIP Code
www.LinkedIn.com/state/susanbjobseeker

---

## FINANCIAL SERVICES PROFILE

Accurate and highly productive Financial Services Manager experienced with leading multi-departmental teams, completing complex financial analysis projects and meeting deadlines. Extensive knowledge of corporate finance and asset management. Capable project manager. Adept at learning and using enterprise financial systems. Core skills include

◆ Financial Reporting ◆ Project Management ◆ Financial Analysis ◆ Forecasting
◆ Software Installations ◆ Teamwork ◆ Corporate Governance ◆ Annual Reports

---

## PROFESSIONAL EXPERIENCE

**Company A,** City, State, 20_ _ – Present
**Financial Services Manager**

- Managed 10-member team of financial analysts that consistently met deadlines and won numerous team bonus awards for exemplary collaborative and technical skills.
- Calculated, summarized and concisely presented monthly forecast and reporting statements exceeding $1.2M to senior management.
- Streamlined receivables process that increased 60, 90 and 120 day cash receipts by 25%.
- Identified programming error in financial accounting system that saved the company $100,000 in first quarter after problem was corrected.
- Analyzed multi-million dollar building operation service contracts, negotiated lower rates, and reduced asset management expenses in two categories by 15%.

**Company B,** City, State, 20_ _ - 20_ _
**Financial Analyst**

- Recognized by two department directors for initiating improvements in revenue, balance statement and budget variance operations.
- Met every deadline for preparing fiscal reports and presenting them to management.
- Conducted an operational procedure analysis and identified new ways to reduce input errors.
- Formed a peer-to-peer mentoring and coaching team that reduced unit turnover by 80%.

---

## EDUCATION

**Master of Business Administration**
State University, School of Business,
Collegetown, State

**Bachelor of Science in Business Administration**
State University, Collegetown, State

---

## TECHNICAL SKILLS

◆ Advanced Microsoft Excel ◆ Advanced IBM SPSS Statistics Professional ◆ SAP
◆ Microsoft Office Word, Power Point, Outlook, SharePoint
◆ Proprietary in-house financial reporting systems ◆ Salesforce

## PLAIN TEXT RESUME — For Web-based Applications

**First name Last name**
City, State, Zip Code
555.555.5555
Firstname.Lastname@gmail.com

**OBJECTIVE**
2nd shift Assembly or Production position

**WORK HISTORY**
General Laborer, 20_ _ - 20_ _          Company A Name          Anytown, Minnesota
- Quickly learned how to operate sophisticated machinery with fast-tracked
  training in the operator's temporary absence
- Met daily shipment quota to shrink wrap, palletize and place product in
  priority spots
- Operated forklift to safely move product pallets to loading dock for waiting
  trucks

Order Picker, 20_ _ - 20_ _          Company B Name          Suburbia, Minnesota
- Accurately filled orders by hand picking products from warehouse inventory
- Recognized by supervisor for consistently exceeding output quotas
- Followed order packing instructions and fragile item protocols

Truck Unloader, 20 _ _ - 20_ _          Company C Name          Big City, Minnesota
- Unloaded merchandise from truck, placed on carts, and delivered to restocker
- Skilled in use of RFID tags, scanners, and inventory control computer
  software
- Used math skills to calculate and complete delivery overage reports

Stock Associate, 20_ _ - 20_ _          Company D Name          Big City, Minnesota
- Reduced turnaround time by 15% for all customer exchanges or returns
- Safely and quickly completed inventory in temperature controlled settings
- Organized work team to check product expiration dates and remove expired
  items

**VOLUNTEER EXPERIENCE**
- Food Sorting Shift          Product Rescue Center          Anytown, Minnesota
- Grocery Floor Assistant     Suburban Area Food Shelf       Suburbia, Minnesota
- Greeter                     County Hospital                Big City, Minnesota

**TRAINING**
- Lean Warehousing 2-day in-service by Company B
- Conveyor and hoist operation and maintenance training by mentor
- Units Moved Workshop - correct use of Track, Trace and Control to reduce costs

**EDUCATION**          Diploma          Jones Thomas High School          Big City, Minnesota

# CHRONOLOGICAL RESUME TEMPLATE

## Your First and Last Name (Use a larger font)

Address, City, State ZIP
Phone Number      (Easiest to reach you and with a professional voice mail greeting.)
Your Email      (Use or create a professional email for use in your job search.)
Your LinkedIn public URL      (Do this only if you have a complete LinkedIn profile.)

## OBJECTIVE

Position title (name of the job you are applying for) **with** (name of company with the job opening) **in** (name of the city and state where the company is located).

## SKILLS SUMMARY

One way to format this section is to list the skills you have that mirror the words used in the employer's job posting. Another format is to group skills under a topic heading. Computer software skills can be part of a skills summary. Use 3 – 5 lines in a resume to summarize your skills.

## WORK EXPERIENCE

### Name of Prior Company, City, State      Year to Year
*Title of Prior Job*

- Keep the number of bullet points about the same for each job. Use more points for your previous job that is most like the job opening.
- Search Onetonline.org using the title of your past job, and find the list of tasks.
- Find tasks you have done in the past. Match these tasks with the qualifications and requirements in the job posting. Do this for each job application.
- Customize your resume for each job application. Include only your past tasks that best match what the employer is asking for in the job posting.
- One line per bullet is ideal, two lines are ok, but you will have fewer points if they are all two lines.
- Start each bullet point with a verb. Follow that with why, how, or what the impact was to the organization.

### Name of Prior Company, City, State      Year to Year
*Title of Prior Job*

- Quantify what you have done such as increased sales 20% in one quarter. Numbers justify your skill level.
- Use present tense OR past tense, i.e. Present vs. Presented. Use one tense throughout your resume.
- Arrange skills in the same order you see in the job posting. Required at the top followed by preferred.
- Feel good about what you are presenting. Be positive about all your skills!

## EDUCATION

### Your Degree or Certification, Your College, City, State (Omit year if more than 5 years)

- Include your GPA if over 3.0 and degree, certification or certificate was completed in last 5 years
- If no degrees keep same format and include how many credits earned or anticipated graduation date.
- If a high school diploma or GED® is your highest education level, be sure to include it. Omit listing your high school if you have attended a post-secondary educational institution.

## AWARDS, CERTIFICATIONS & ADDITIONAL TRAINING

(List training, awards and certifications that best match the job opening requirements.)

- ACT's National Career Readiness Certificate (NCRC) Silver Level      Year
- Forklift Certified      Year

# CHRONOLOGICAL RESUME

# Mike Manufacturing

905 Assembly Street, Anytown, MN 55350
123-456-7890
MikeManufacturing@email.com
www.linkedin.com/mn/mikemanufacturing

## OBJECTIVE

Production Technician with Anytown Precision Manufacturing Company in Anytown, Minnesota.

## SKILLS SUMMARY

| Manufacturing Production | Read and Interpret | Computer |
|---|---|---|
| Kaizen, Lean, 5S | Blueprints | Microsoft Office – Word, Excel, Outlook |
| Shop Floor Control | Schematics | CAD output |
| Materials Flow | Process Control Charts | MRP |

## WORK EXPERIENCE

**Technology, Inc.,** Anytown, Minnesota — 2011 – Present
*Assembly Process Specialist*

- Reduced downtime by 30% after analysis of normal and abnormal conditional trends using SPC and problem solving techniques.
- Applied Kaizen principles to streamline input communication process with maintenance and engineering.
- Implemented a troubleshooting process to identify, document and understand equipment problems.
- Formed a process and safety resource team. Improved safety record by 12% in first year.
- Recommended more efficient method to verify specifications of process with engineering department.

**Custom Production, Inc.,** Somewhere, Minnesota — 2007 – 2011
*Production Operator*

- Operated machines that produced foam and rubber products and prototype molds.
- Decreased rejections by 30% after improving the die cleaning process.
- Received numerous awards for completing work orders before deadline to guarantee on time delivery.
- Used blueprint reading and interpretation skills to determine customer specifications and ensure quality.

**Assembly Manufacturing Company,** Lakes, Minnesota — 2003 – 2007
*Mechanical Assembler*

- Assembled drive gear components using hand and semiautomatic hand tools.
- Operated machines that stamped and fabricated parts that met blueprint and customer specifications.
- Conducted inspection of final parts. Record of meeting company standards for quality and defects.
- Maintained a perfect safety record by following all safety policies and procedures.

## EDUCATION

**Anytown High School,** Anytown, MN, High School Diploma

## AWARDS, CERTIFICATIONS & ADDITIONAL TRAINING

- National Career Readiness Certificate, *(NCRC) Silver #G12TJDGHHI* — 2014
- Forklift Operation Certification, *30 hour course, OSHA* — 2011

## 1-PAGE SKILLS RESUME TEMPLATE

### Your First and Last Name
Address, City, State, ZIP
Phone Number
Email Address

---

### OBJECTIVE

Position title (name of the job you are applying for) with (name of company with the job opening)
in (name of the city and state where the company is located).

---

### PROFESSIONAL EXPERIENCE

*SKILL AREA ONE*
- Pick 3 - 6 of your skills and the corresponding accomplishment statements that best match the job-posting announcement.
- Look at the first skill or requirement that you see in the job posting. What you see first is often the most important qualification or skill that the employer wants to find when they advertise a job opening.
- Check out www.OnetOnline.org if you need helpful lists of the tasks, tools and technology, knowledge, skills and abilities and work activities for your current or previous job titles.

*SKILL AREA TWO*
- Place your strongest skill at the top of each Skill Area section.
- Use relevant information from any job that you listed in your employment history.
- Do not include a Skill Area that is not supported by past employment.

*SKILL AREA THREE*
- A resume is a marketing tool, a personal "brochure." Make it easy to read and understand.
- Avoid uncommon acronyms. The hiring decision maker that reads your resume must quickly understand what you have to offer, your experience, your skills and your qualifications.
- Start each statement with a verb that shows the reader what you did, why you did it or what your results were.

---

### EMPLOYMENT HISTORY

(Typically, go back no more than 10 years for your employment history.
Include jobs back to 15 years if they are relevant to the job opening or you need the years of experience to be qualified.)

| | |
|---|---|
| *Job Title*, Company Name, City, ST | YEAR – YEAR |
| *Job Title*, Company Name, City, ST | YEAR – YEAR |
| *Job Title*, Company Name, City, ST | YEAR – YEAR |

---

### EDUCATION

Your Degree, Certification or Certificate, Your College, City, State (Omit year if more than 5 years)
- Include your GPA if over 3.0 and degree, certification or certificate was completed in last 5 years
- If no degrees keep same format and include how many credits earned or anticipated graduation date.
- If a high school diploma or GED® is your highest education level, be sure to include it. Omit listing your high school if you have attended a post-secondary educational institution.

---

### AWARDS, CERTIFICATIONS & ADDITIONAL TRAINING

(List company sponsored training, awards or certifications that best match the job opening requirements.)

# 1-PAGE SKILLS RESUME

## Bill Buyer

1160 Saddleridge Court, Watertown City, MN 12345
320-000-0000
billthebuyer@email.com
www.linkedin.com/mn/billbuyer

### OBJECTIVE

Purchasing Agent with The Parts Company in Watertown City, Minnesota.

### PROFESSIONAL EXPERIENCE

*INVENTORY MANAGEMENT*

- Meet internal and external customer same day demands by ensuring materials are in stock.
- Awarded performance bonus for maintaining meticulous inventory and sales records.
- Prepare purchase orders for over 12,000 stock-keeping units (SKUs).
- Administer procurement and resolve shipping errors.
- Assist with preparation of annual inventory budget in excess of $1M. Obtain owner approval.

*ACCOUNTING*

- Record daily and monthly transactions for accurate receipt and disbursement information.
- Administer customer leases, monthly billing statements, and late payment fees.
- Negotiate contracts, fees, and authorize payment.
- Manage receivable balance, administer collections, and monitor cash flow.
- Analyze and present financial reports to onsite management and off-site ownership.

*CUSTOMER SERVICE COMMUNICATION SKILLS*

- Assess, recommend and help locate products and materials to satisfy customer needs.
- Respond to customer inquiries in-person, by phone, or by email.
- Resolve difficult sales and product performance situations to maintain excellent customer satisfaction while meeting company margin goals.

*COMPUTER SKILLS*

- Advanced Microsoft Office Excel skills, and proficient in Word, Power Point and Outlook.
- Use Customer Relationship Management (CRM) — Salesforce.com® to personally respond to customer inquiries and document actions taken.
- Desktop and mobile Internet Procurement and Order Processing System — JD Edwards.

### EMPLOYMENT HISTORY

| | |
|---|---|
| *Inventory Control Specialist,* Distribution, Inc., Somewhere, MN | 2013 – Current |
| *Apartment Property Manager,* Lloyd Management, Collegetown, MN | 2010 – 2012 |
| *Parts Associate,* Value Auto Parts, Collegetown, MN | 2009 – 2011 |

### EDUCATION

| | |
|---|---|
| *Associate of Applied Science in Accounting (A.A.S) degree*<br>Central College, Collegetown, Minnesota | 2012 |

### AWARDS, CERTIFICATIONS & ADDITIONAL TRAINING

| | |
|---|---|
| *National Career Readiness Certificate (NCRC),* Gold Certification #GHH596Q | 2013 |
| *Team of the Year* – national achievement award to recognize sales increases | 2010 |

## 2-PAGE RESUME EXAMPLE

# First M. Combotwo

233 2nd Avenue South
Minneapolis, MN 55423

612-123-4567
first_last@yahoo.com

### SUMMARY

Executive Assistant with a decade of C-Suite clerical and administrative services experience.
Energetic, flexible and self-motivated. Excellent interpersonal communication abilities.
Proven organizational and planning expertise; works with minimal supervision.
Excellent customer service skills.

### QUALIFICATIONS

- MS Office Word, Excel, Outlook and SharePoint
- Type over 50 WPM
- Excellent verbal and written communication skills

- Safeguard confidential information
- Establish and maintain positive client relationships
- Independent judgment and discretion

- Problem solver
- Organized with keen attention to detail
- Sales, special events and marketing support

### ACCOMPLISHMENTS

Administrative Support

- Provided four person senior executive team with timely and accurate response to clerical, scheduling, travel, and report generation needs.
- Administered purchase orders for the marketing, travel and special event budgets for an eight-state region.
- Negotiated office supply and equipment services with vendors that resulted in a 20% annual decrease in this expense category.

Organizational Skills

- Reduced employee turnover by 10% after development of a faster expense reimbursement process. Other offices replicated this procedure and had similar results.
- Expedited the turnaround of incoming and outgoing correspondence by creating a new internal communication center.
- Increased margin after development of a multi-department regional facility to centralize the purchasing and distribution of promotional items. Inventory availability increased and the cost per item decreased.

## 2-PAGE RESUME EXAMPLE *(CONTINUED)*

### SALES, MARKETING AND SPECIAL EVENTS

- Generated increased product use after developing and coordinating a hands-on and interactive software training event.

- Supported the new product roll out team at national trade shows. Our team consistently exceeded its sales goals by more than a million dollars.

- Coordinated two regional strategy planning meetings and conferences for both internal and external customers. Made certain that all participants arrived on time, had appropriate accommodations, and positive team experiences.

### OPERATIONS / LOGISTICS

- Coordinated regional office facilities logistics with corporate staff and building property management. Completed five suburban office park renovations and expanded two production facilities. Met company business continuation needs during each transition. Created and wrote a daily newsletter to keep executives and staff informed during each project.

- Recruited, hired and supervised temporary support personnel for special projects and events.

- Managed special event expenses by carefully assessing needs, evaluating expenses, and monitoring equipment rental.

### PROFESSIONAL EXPERIENCE

| Company | Company | Company |
|---|---|---|
| Minnetonka, MN | Bloomington, MN | New Hope, MN |
| 2008-2014 | 2006-2008 | 2003-2006 |
| Executive Assistant | Administrative Assistant | Office Coordinator |

### RECOGNITIONS AND AWARDS

- Recognized as "Support Team Member of the Year"
- Won "Contributor of the Quarter Award" three times in 2½ years
- Winner of the "Impact" award for facilities management

### EDUCATION

**State University, Central City, MN**                    2000-2002
Completed 60 semester hours toward bachelor's degree in English

## SCHOOL-TO-WORK CHRONOLOGICAL

# ELIZABETH JONES

000 Ames Drive • Eden Prairie, Minnesota 55347

(952) 123-4567 • jones@umn.edu

### OBJECTIVE

A public relations position using my skills in writing, graphic design, web design, marketing and social media.

### SKILLS

*Promotion:* Twin Cities label marketing for Chicago-based Aware Records.

*Media:* Interned with two corporations writing press releases and helping develop marketing strategies.

*Social Media:* Created, promoted and provided content for a blog focused on the local music scene.

*Research:* Keen understanding of pop culture, current pop issues and evolving trends.

### EMPLOYMENT HISTORY

*Compellent Technologies*
June 20__ – September 20__
Research Intern, Marketing Intern

*Best Buy*
January 20__ – November 20__
Media Sales Associate

### PUBLIC RELATIONS EXPERIENCE

*Come Pick Me Up*
January 20__ – Present
www.comepickmeup.net
Creator, Writer, Developer
Live show reviews, new band features, music news.

## SCHOOL-TO-WORK CHRONOLOGICAL *(CONTINUED)*

*Aware Records*
Chicago, Illinois
Summer 20__– Present
Label Rep — Responsible for marketing a roster of music artist
and Aware products by using a variety of materials for both
grassroots marketing and online promotions.

*AjiSignal.com*
August 20__ – December 20__
Staff Writer — Wrote weekly articles, such as new band
features or show reviews, about music related happenings in
the Twin Cities.

*The Music, The Message*
February 20__ – January 20__
(formerly EmotionalPunk.com)
Staff Writer — Reviewed records, conducted band interviews
with both major label and independent artists, live show
reviews.

**EDUCATION**

*University of Minnesota,* Minneapolis, Minnesota
Bachelor of Arts, Journalism
Major: Professional Strategic Communication
Minor: New Media Studies
GPA: 3.75

*University of St. Thomas,* St. Paul, Minnesota
Completed 30 credits
GPA: 3.93

*City University London*
Semester Abroad — Journalism
London, United Kingdom

*University of Westminster*
Semester Abroad — Digital Media and Communications
London, United Kingdom

# TRANSFERRING MILITARY SKILLS

| IN THE MILITARY | IN THE CIVILIAN WORLD |
| --- | --- |
| AAM-ARCOM | award/recognition |
| battalion | division |
| brigade | group/division |
| combat | conflict/emergency |
| commander | director/senior management/president |
| company | company/unit department |
| Executive Officer | deputy director/assistant |
| Field grade officer | executive manager |
| First Sergeant | personnel manager |
| garrison | organization/company |
| leader | supervisor/manager |
| medal | award/recognition |
| Military Occupation Specialty (MOS) | career specialty |
| mission | task/function/objective |
| NCO | supervisor/manager |
| OER/NCOER | performance rating/evaluation |
| Operations NCO | operations manager |
| Personnel Actions Center (PAC) | personnel office |
| Platoon Sergeant | supervisor/instructor/trainer |
| PLDC/BNCOC | leadership/advanced leadership development course |
| reconnaissance | data collection/survey/analysis |
| regulations | policy/guidelines/instructions |
| Senior NCO's | director/first-line supervisor |
| Senior Field Grade Officer | senior administrator/chief executive/department head/ program director/deputy chief/senior executive |
| Sergeant Major | senior advisor |
| squad | section |
| Squad Leader | team leader/team chief |
| subordinates | employees/personnel/staff |
| Supply Sergeant | supply manager/logistics manager |
| TDA/MTOE | organizational structure/human and material resources |
| temporary duty (TDY) | business trip/temporary duty |
| Uniform Code of Military Justice (UCMJ) | legal action/legal document |
| War College | Advanced Strategic Studies Course |
| Warrant Officers | director/specialist/department manager |

## MILITARY TO CIVILIAN RESUME

# John A. Military

123 Main Street, #301
Maple Grove, MN 55330
763-555-0400
Email: johnamilitary@email.com

### OBJECTIVE

Military veteran seeks Correctional Officer position with Jefferson County Corrections.

### SUMMARY OF SKILLS

- Calm under stress
- Physically and mentally in shape
- Excellent oral and written communication skills
- Tactful customer service
- Trusted and reliable team member
- Write accurate computer-based reports

- First responder emergency experience
- Incident coordination of 20 – 100 personnel
- Vehicle mobilization, operation and pursuit in various weather conditions
- Use, maintenance and storage of weapons valued in excess of $1.5M

### WORK EXPERIENCE

**Military Police/Security Patrol**, U.S. Army, Iraq and Afghanistan, June 2007–June 2013

- Provided digital information, industrial facilities, personnel, resource and infrastructure security
- Trained and experienced at administering Advanced First Aid
- Conducted investigations and interrogations

- Utilized established procedures and techniques for data and evidence collection and processing
- Directed crime scene security and processed individuals
- Detained criminal suspects

### EDUCATION and TRAINING

- **United States Army Military Police School** — Fort Leonard Wood, Missouri

  *Certifications*
  - Advanced First Aid
  - Basic combat skills and use of firearms
  - Investigating and collecting evidence

  *Training*
  - Laws and jurisdiction
  - Traffic and crowd control
  - Arrest and restraint of suspects

- **Thomas Jefferson High School** — Sometown, MN

  *High School Diploma*

# Cover Letter Formats

Many employers will first ask you to fill out an application and submit a resume. While the cover letter may have diminished somewhat in importance, it does not mean you shouldn't take the care to write a good one. Here is an overview and a few examples of cover letters.

## GENERAL OUTLINE

Your Name
Street Address
City, State Zip Code
Phone Number
Email Address

Date

Individual's Name
Job Title
Name of Organization
Street Address
City, State Zip Code

Dear Mr./Ms. Employer:

First Paragraph: State the reason for writing. Name the specific position or type of work for which you're applying. Mention how you learned of the opening.

Second Paragraph: Explain why you're interested in working for this employer and specify how you're PERFECT for this position. Don't repeat the information on your resume. Include something special or unique about yourself that will benefit the employer. Remember, the reader will consider this an example of your writing skills.

Third Paragraph: Mention your resume is enclosed and indicate your desire to meet with the employer. You may want to suggest alternate dates and times, or simply advise them of your flexibility to the time and place. Include contact information where you can be easily reached. Include a statement or question that will encourage the reader to respond. Be sure to communicate your plan to follow up. Finally, thank the employer for his/her time.

Sincerely,


(Your signature in blue or black ink)
Your typed name

Enclosure

# "T" COVER LETTER FORMAT

Molly McGinnis
18881 No Name Trail, Lakeville, MN 55044
(952) 123-4567, molly.mcginnis@ymail.com

January 4, 20__

Travelers Insurance
Human Resource Department
One Tower Square
Hartford, CT 06183

Dear Human Resource:

I am very interested in the open Workers Compensation Case Manager position located in St. Paul, Minn., advertised on your company website on January 4, 20__. Having related experience in the medical, legal and business industry makes me a qualified candidate for your needs.

| Your Needs | My Qualifications |
| --- | --- |
| • Workers compensation experience | • High volume workers compensation claims |
| • Management of files | • File management/ case management |
| • Claim resolution | • Handled resolution 150+ files |
| • Negotiation/settlements | • Evaluation of claim settlement |

To aid your efforts in qualifying possible candidates, I have attached a detailed resume for your review. I am confident you will find my background and experience an excellent match for the talents you are seeking. I welcome the opportunity to speak with you in person about my qualifications and look forward to your response. Thank you for your consideration.

Sincerely,

Molly McGinnis
Encl.

## JOB MATCH COVER LETTER

**Corrine Johnson**
10936 Fillmore St. NE • Blaine, Minnesota 55434 • 612.123.4567
CJohnson_277@msn.com

December 22, 20_ _

Minnesota Historical Society
Human Resources Department
345 Kellogg Blvd. W.
St. Paul, MN 55102

Dear Human Resources Representative:

I am very interested in the position of Editor and creating the Minnesota Encyclopedia. You indicated that your team is looking for someone with the ability to:

- **Coordinate project activities of the Minnesota Encyclopedia**
  From idea inception to publication, my three-person acquisitions team coordinated every aspect of our book publishing projects.

- **Perform content editing**
  I have nine years of experience editing and publishing books, journal articles and white papers.

- **Develop professional relationships with colleagues, authors and publishers**
  My commitment to quality, integrity and the reader has connected me with colleagues, authors and publishers.

- **Organize own time well, coordinate multiple projects**
  Experienced with managing three to four simultaneous projects and building trust within a team to complete each project on deadline.

I have what it takes to create the Minnesota Encyclopedia on time and on budget. I am an excellent candidate for this position and would welcome an opportunity to discuss my skills in person. I love Minnesota history and have visited many of the state's historical sites and museums. Thank you for your consideration.

Sincerely,

Corrine Johnson
Enclosure

## JOB MATCH COVER LETTER

Your Name
Address
City, State, Zip Code
Phone Number
Email Address

February 25, 20__

Ms. Jane Smith, Title
Work Incorporated
555 Pine Street
St. Paul, MN 55555

Dear Ms. Smith:

The position of Administrative Assistant listed in the Daily Tribune on February 24, 20__, caught my attention. The skills and qualifications you require closely match my experience in this career field.

- ***Detail-oriented, experienced Administrative Assistant:***
  Four years Administrative Assistant experience with responsibility for numerous detailed reports.

- ***Assist Customer Relations Manager:***
  Worked with our Customer Relations Manager for two years.

- ***Corporate experience with major clients:***
  Regularly served purchasing agents at Fortune 500 companies.

- ***PC knowledge:***
  Mastery of the entire Microsoft Office Suite.

Enclosed is my resume for your review and consideration. I believe I am an excellent candidate for this position and look forward to meeting with you to discuss it in greater detail. I will call you to determine when an interview might be possible. Thank you.

Sincerely,


(Signature)
Typed Name

Enclosure

# INVITED COVER LETTER

Johnny Network
678 River Drive
Somewhere, MN 55555
(555) 555-5555
Johnny.Network@fakemail.com


June 26, 20__

Mr. Phillip Morework
Production Manager
XYZ Corporation
21 Industry Lane
Anytown, MN 55555

Dear Mr. Morework:

Please consider my qualifications for the Lead Production Assistant opportunity, which was posted on your website on June 20, 20__. With a proven high-tech background in Fortune 100 companies, I am well qualified and eager to represent your company in this capacity.

Environments that are fast paced, require multi-tasking and value production deadlines are where I thrive. In relation to leadership, I have been responsible for up to 35 staff members and have built a reputation for making quality administrative decisions in a fair and consistent manner. Constant negotiations with all levels of management and staff have strengthened my interpersonal skills.

Enclosed is my resume, and I am looking forward to discussing my potential with you. I will call you to confirm receipt of this information and to discuss possible next steps. Thank you very much for your time and consideration.

Sincerely,


Johnny Network

Enclosure

**INVITED COVER LETTER** — **No Paid-Work Experience**

Wanda Job
5555 Lakewood Road
Somewhere, MN 55555
(555) 555-5555
wandajob@fakemail.com

January 6, 20__

Ms. Marilyn Payer
Housekeeping Manager
Rodetown Inn
123 Indiana Drive
Anytown, MN 55555

Dear Ms. Payer:

Your ad for a Housekeeper in the Jobs Now newspaper on Sunday, January 4, 20__, caught my attention. With over 10 years of housekeeping and home maintenance experience, I believe that I have the necessary skills for the position. My resume is enclosed for your consideration.

Rodetown Inn has an excellent reputation in the community as a quality employer, and my skills perfectly match the requirements. Having been a homeowner for more than five years, I do all of my own maintenance and repair. For the past three years I have been a home care volunteer for the Salvation Army's "Be Friends" program. This includes helping disabled and elderly persons with household chores such as: bed-making, cleaning, vacuuming, dusting, doing laundry, washing walls and windows, mopping, mowing, raking and shoveling. Several patrons have commended me for being extremely reliable, efficient, organized and a good team worker.

This opportunity to apply my skills in a new environment is exciting to me. It would be beneficial for us to meet to discuss the position and my qualifications in greater detail. I will contact you to determine when a convenient interview time might be arranged. Please feel free to contact me in the interim at the number shown above. Thank you for your time. I look forward to talking with you soon.

Sincerely,


Wanda Job
Enclosure

## REFERRAL COVER LETTER

Susan Jones
444 Canoe Bay Trail
Somewhere, MN 55555
(555) 555-5555
SJones@fakemail.com

July 31, 20__

Ms. Rhonda Leland
Corporate Manager
Doneright Corporation
42 Industry Circle
Somewhere Else, MN 55555

Dear Ms. Leland:

Mary Smith, Vice President of Marketing with Doneright Corporation, suggested that I contact you directly regarding my interest in an Administrative Assistant position with your organization. Although my resume is actively on file in Human Resources, Ms. Smith felt that you would want to be made aware of my unique qualifications and availability. Enclosed is a copy of my resume for your consideration.

My solid background makes me a highly qualified Administrative Assistant. With more than four years of experience in executive management for a large manufacturing company, I have mastered the skills necessary to succeed at Doneright. My qualifications include extensive PC experience with the software used at Doneright Corp. (Microsoft Office Suite), proven customer service skills, itinerary planning and report writing.

I will be in your area on August 20, 20__, between 9 a.m. and 3 p.m., and would appreciate an opportunity to meet with you to discuss my qualifications in greater detail. I plan to contact you to arrange a possible meeting time.

Thank you for your time and consideration.

Sincerely,


Susan Jones

Enclosure

c: M. Smith

## COLD-CONTACT COVER LETTER

Karen Kareer
456 Pond View Road
Somewhere, MN 55555
(555) 555-5555
kkareer@fakemail.com

May 20, 20_ _

Ms. Francisca Favor
Department Manager
EFTG Industries, Inc.
210 Industry Avenue
Anytown, MN 55555

Dear Ms. Favor:

As you know, innovation and new ways of thinking are important to a company's success. With my history of marketing achievement, I have proven to be an excellent communicator as well as a valuable innovator. This letter is in regard to my strong interest in your company and my desire to contribute to its success.

Presently, I am marketing computer products for a major supplier using online, television and news advertising. My supervisors have commended me for finding creative ways to spend less money and receive greater return.

Enclosed is my resume for your review and consideration. EFTG Industries has a reputation for excellence. I would like the opportunity to use my talents to market your quality line of technical products. I will call you to further discuss my qualifications and how I can benefit your company. If you prefer, you may reach me in the evenings at (555) 555-5555.

Thank you for your time. I look forward to meeting you.

Sincerely,



Karen Kareer

Enclosure

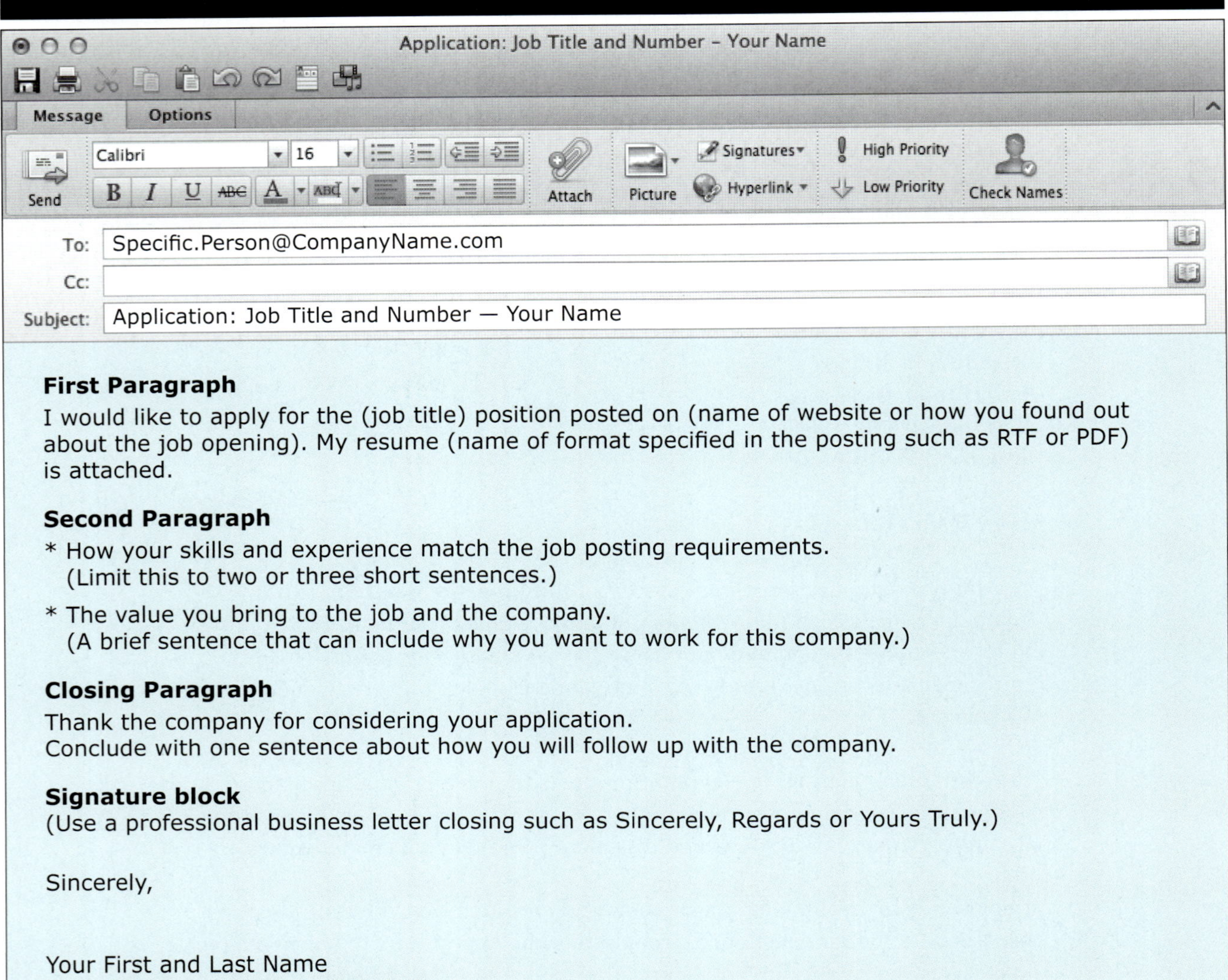

# EMAIL COVER LETTER



**First Paragraph**
I would like to apply for the (job title) position posted on (name of website or how you found out about the job opening). My resume (name of format specified in the posting such as RTF or PDF) is attached.

**Second Paragraph**
* How your skills and experience match the job posting requirements.
  (Limit this to two or three short sentences.)

* The value you bring to the job and the company.
  (A brief sentence that can include why you want to work for this company.)

**Closing Paragraph**
Thank the company for considering your application.
Conclude with one sentence about how you will follow up with the company.

**Signature block**
(Use a professional business letter closing such as Sincerely, Regards or Yours Truly.)

Sincerely,


Your First and Last Name
Your Address, City, State ZIP Code
Your email address

## Email Cover Letter Tips

- Do not repeat information on your resume or say "see resume."

- Do not use text language abbreviations in a job application cover letter.

- Keep all sentences short. You may want to limit each sentence to no more than 10 words.

- Send a sample email to yourself or to friends to see what your email letter looks like on a smartphone or tablet screen. Even if the reader is viewing your letter on a computer monitor, it's a good bet that they are using half or less of the screen.

- Attach your resume in the format requested. Plain Text File (RTF), PDF and Microsoft Word are the most commonly requested formats.

- Rename your resume before you attach it to the email application letter. Use your name and the posted job title or number such as JSmith. MarketingDirector.MD12345.

- A company may ask for your resume in an email format. Cut and paste your resume into your email program and format it. Check the appearance by emailing it to yourself before you send it to the employer.

- If required by the company, confirm that you have completed their online job application.

- Use the spell check feature on your email program and proof your email twice before you hit "Send."

# CHAPTER 5

# Applications, References and Portfolios

*"The closest to perfection a person ever comes is when he fills out a job application form."*

— STANLEY J. RANDALL, WRITER

A necessary part of every job pursuit is the job application. It's an online or paper form requiring you to fill out information illustrating your career, education and qualifications. It can be a tedious process without the right preparation because it requires a great deal of detail, from dates of employment to addresses and supervisors. Correctly completing an application should not be underestimated since some employers require you to submit one before they will look at your resume or cover letter.

Applications will be studied and compared with other job seekers by human resource personnel, hiring managers, division heads and, at larger companies, applicant tracking software. The document provides another opportunity to sell yourself to potential employers and offer a good first impression.

Online job applications are popular with employers because they are easier to manage. Many employers will ask you to complete an application prior to their staffs even glancing at your resume or cover letter. Why? When several people apply for the same position employers can pre-screen applicants by using automated assessments done by applicant tracking software.

## GUIDELINES FOR APPLICATIONS

Applications require a lot of details: personal information, dates of previous jobs, former supervisors, reasons for leaving jobs and skills you have developed throughout your career. We have tips to help you organize and standardize this information.

### Creating a Personal Data Record

Several strategies can help shorten the time required to complete applications. Once you have the basic information collected, you only have to repurpose it again — and again and again. Start by creating a Personal Data Record. This will have your job career history and personal information in an online or paper file.

# TIPS FOR COMPLETING AN APPLICATION

- Never use abbreviations, slang or emoticons (those online symbols for a person's mood or expression).

- Do not write "see resume" on sites requesting that you attach a resume since applicant tracking systems may not understand that phrase. Fill out the entire application.

- For paper applications keep your Personal Data Record available so you avoid making errors. Print clearly in black ink, do not use abbreviations and respond to all questions. Use N/A (not applicable) if the section does not apply to you.

- Be positive and honest while avoiding any negative information that may show you are not the right person for the job. And keep in mind false information can become the basis for dismissal.

- You may come across applications containing illegal and tricky questions. These may include questions about age, gender, sexual orientation, disabilities, health, marital status, children, race, arrests or convictions, religion and workers' compensation. Use N/A or a dash to answer. Additional information about illegal questions can be found at a Minnesota WorkForce Center, the state Attorney General's Office or the state Human Rights Office.

- If you have a felony and are applying for a job in a state such as Minnesota that has a Ban the Box law, you will not be asked about your criminal history because employers are required to remove questions about it, postponing such queries until later in the hiring process.

- If you are applying for a job in a state that hasn't passed a Ban the Box law and have a felony, you should make the effort to meet the employer before submitting your application. This gives you a chance to sell your skills, enthusiasm and other qualities before managers learn about your offense.

- Target your qualifications since many application forms have limited space to display your skills, experience and accomplishments. List your qualifications that match the specific needs of the job. If possible show knowledge of the employer and its products or services.

- When applying for advertised jobs or for specific positions, make sure to enter the correct job title in the blank space provided. When you aren't applying for a specific position, state the name of the department in which you wish to work. (If you have an interest in more than one advertised job, you might have to fill out more than one application.)

- If you have job gaps in your employment history, try listing positive ways you spent time while unemployed. Make your answer short, simple and truthful. Examples include managing and maintaining a household, volunteering, attending school and providing child care. If you volunteered for an organization make note of the type of work you did.

- When asked about salary requirements give a range or respond with "negotiable." Use one of these responses even if you know the wage. You never know what the future holds, and you could negotiate a higher salary. Find salary ranges at www.iseek.org, www. careeronestop.org or www.bls.gov.

Preferably, you should have your data record as an ASCII (plain text) file because you can then simply cut and paste the information into applications as you fill them out. Another time-saving device is the "auto-fill" feature available on Firefox and as part of Google's toolbar. The built-in function allows you to fill out personal data once and then have it automatically populate online applications and other Web-based forms.

So, what information do you need for most applications?

Obviously, be ready with your name, address, phone numbers (business, home, fax and mobile) and email address. Then, collect your career information — your past four jobs (or more or less), the addresses and phone numbers of those companies, your managers in each of those positions and their phone numbers.

You will need the month and year you started working, when you left and the reasons for your departures. Write a brief description of your duties for each position, too, because most applications include a place for that information.

Additionally, you should collect information on your degrees, certifications, honors, special training, hobbies, volunteer activities and other relevant experience that could help win you a job. For a more thorough list of what might be required, head for the Personal Data Record document at the end of this chapter.

## Dealing With "Reason for Leaving"

Explaining why you left an employer can be a sensitive topic. Saying you hated your boss or the firm had a work environment akin to a prison are probably not good options. Reasons for leaving can be a tough part of the application to fill in truthfully without having your application and resume rejected by potential employers.

When responding to "reasons for leaving" choose your words carefully because negative responses may provide an easy way for the employer to eliminate you from consideration. When stating why you left a job avoid using the words "fired," "quit," "illness" or "personal reasons" because those responses may reduce your chances of being called for an interview. Always look for positive statements. You could say, for example, you returned to school to learn new skills or to find a job that more closely matched your skills.

If you were "fired" don't use that word or "terminated." Find a phrase that sounds neutral such as "involuntary separation." And then call past employers and negotiate what they will say in response to reference checks. When contacting former employers, reintroduce yourself and explain you are looking for a new job. For legal reasons chances are good they will not tell future employers you were fired, and you can ask that they simply provide your dates of employment, your job title and a description of your job duties.

Should you face termination in the future you should request that the employer's records reveal a mutually agreeable reason for separation.
You don't want to hurt your future employment opportunities, and your employer may feel the same way. After all, people are asked to leave for any number of reasons that have little to do with their job abilities and more to do with a poor job match or poor fit with an organization's culture.

Have you quit a job? Be prepared to offer an explanation. If you left under less than favorable conditions, avoid saying anything negative about the employer and use terms such as "resigned,"

## HOW TO ATTACH A RESUME TO AN ONLINE APPLICATION

Some online applications require you to electronically attach your resume and will specify the format — MS Word, PDF or ASCII-Plain Text. If you don't have a computer, buy a USB flash drive and save a copy of your resume (in each format) to it.

Another option is opening a free account at Google Docs, which offers several online applications that mirror Microsoft's Office Suite. Google has helpful videos and good explanations on its site describing how to use its Office Suite and how to share content with other users.

Otherwise here's the process, and keep in mind these instructions will vary based on the application you are filling out and the software on your computer. Some job sites and employers will want you to paste your resume into an email. To do this in Windows, use your cursor and highlight your entire resume, right click to "copy" the contents and then go to your email. Place the cursor beneath your open email message, right click and "paste" the resume into it. You can also attach your resume file to an email by clicking on attach file paper clip icon on the toolbar of an open email. When you locate your resume file, click "ok" or "insert." You know your file is attached to the email correctly if you can see the file name listed below the subject of your email.

It's common for online applications to prompt you to attach your resume to the application itself. Usually they will provide a button on the application that links directly to your computer files. Just like attaching a resume to an email, locate the correct file and click "ok" or "insert." Again, you will know the file is attached if you see the file name inserted in the application.

If you're struggling, simply go to the help button and type in "attachments" for step-by-step instructions on how to do it.

"wasn't a good fit" or "voluntarily separated," which imply you followed proper procedures in leaving the job. Other reasons for quitting a job include volunteer work (state what kind of work and with whom you did volunteer work), starting your own business, a scholarship or raising your family. In all of these cases, you need to assure the employer you're now fully ready to assume the responsibilities of a new job.

If you resigned for a better job, that statement better be true. That could include leaving for advancement potential, to work closer to home, to have a better work environment, higher pay or for a career change. Make certain the reason "for a better job" shows no noticeable break in employment that might raise a red flag to hiring managers who may suspect an exaggeration in the statement.

"Quitting to move to another area" for family, greater economic potential or suitability for raising children is a fine reason, but try to use it just once. If that's the reason for several job jumps you may come off as not being a dependable or stable employee. Leaving to attend school is a good enough reason, yet again make sure your application and/or resume agree. You should assure the employer any continuing school activities won't interfere with the job.

Millions of Americans have been laid off through no fault of their own. Those circumstances can be explained with phrases such as "lack of work," "lack of operating funds," "temporary employment," "seasonal employment," "company closed," "plant closing," "company downsizing" or "corporate merger." Layoffs have been such a common aspect of the employment landscape that hiring managers will not hold it against applicants since many of them — or their family members — have suffered the same fate.

In the economy of the last two decades many people have been employed in several jobs. It's no longer a shame to have a portfolio of different jobs and careers. There are employers who appreciate a reservoir of experience and understand a job market where rapid transformation and consolidation have left many workers with few options other than changing jobs.

## GATHERING SUPPORTIVE DOCUMENTS

Aside from resumes and cover letters, which are discussed in Chapter 4, you should have another digital or paper folder with the following elements: recommendations, performance evaluations, references, work samples and portfolios. We explore each of those subjects in the following section.

### Letters of Recommendation

Letters of recommendation are written evaluations of your work performance and work habits. Your present or previous supervisor, manager or team member usually writes them at your request. Employers have no obligation to write these recommendations and may not due to liability issues and company policy, but they may offer a reference letter if you have been a good employee.

If you are a student and have little or no work experience, you can ask your instructor, internship supervisor, adviser, mentor, coach or volunteer coordinator to write letters of recommendation. Without much work experience, especially in jobs meaningful to their careers, students will find the best method of demonstrating their skills may be through having others attest to them in letters of recommendation.

If you are new to the labor market with no paid-work experience, you can ask neighbors, volunteer coordinators, community leaders, congregation members or anyone else who knows you and your work ethic to write a letter of recommendation. The employer will wish to know how long the person has known you, the quality of your work or participation, dedication, skills and work habits.

Don't be surprised if a busy reference asks you to write the first draft of the letter before it is edited and signed. It's a common practice, and feel free to oblige by highlighting in the letter your skills and achievements while working in that job or internship. The reference has the right to add or edit out anything that is not correct before signing it.

## Performance Evaluation

A performance evaluation is a formal, written review or evaluation of your work. It usually covers a specific period of time and includes the quality, quantity, work habits and attitude with which you have performed your job. It can also state your promotions, demotions and reprimands. Positive performance evaluations can be included with your resume or application to bolster your credentials and increase your opportunities of securing a job.

## References

Choose your references with care. Someone influential in your community or in a well-known business may be an effective reference but should not be selected for this reason alone. Look for people who honestly know you and will speak objectively. Avoid references, such as your spouse or a parent, where the potential employer may assume bias.

Avoid references that may be controversial or may concern employers. Examples of these types of references are clergy or social workers. You may even want to use different references for different employment opportunities.

Generally speaking, four types of references can be called upon for recommendations.

- *Work Related*: Includes past employers, coworkers, subordinates or clients who can speak about your specific employment experience. You can also list the people for whom you perform volunteer activities, babysitting, lawn mowing and other odd jobs.

- *Professional*: People who know you on a professional basis such as contacts from business and sales, clubs, or professional and community organizations.

- *Academic*: Instructors and vocational counselors who can speak about your academic endeavors (appropriate for current students or recent graduates).

- *Personal*: Only use a personal reference if you have no work-related, professional or academic ones to offer. Friends and neighbors who know you personally and who can describe your self-management skills are effective. Use the names of people who can tell an employer you can be depended on to do a good job.

When using people as references, get their permission first and tell them about your job search and the type of job opportunities you seek. Don't blindside them. Ask if they would be comfortable recommending you.

Find out if references would prefer to be contacted at work or home. Find out the best time to reach them so this information can be given to a prospective employer. For each reference, you may need to provide the person's occupation and phone number, how long you've known each other and the nature of the relationship.

Send your references a thank you note when you know they have given you a recommendation.

## WORK SAMPLES AND PORTFOLIOS

You probably heard in school the old saying "show, don't tell" or "A picture is worth a thousand words." Those sayings even make sense when considering the possibilities for showcasing your qualifications. Presenting a picture of your work accomplishments may provide immediate impact and understanding of your skills.

Today, work samples and portfolios are a major asset for most job seekers, regardless of their career field. If you have a job where you produce something, even a haircut, you can show photographic evidence of your ability. If you do not have evidence it may be time to start using your smartphone or camera to capture images of your work. A chef or baker can show photographs of culinary creations.

Once you have the photos, share them on social media websites such as Pinterest or Facebook. And don't stop with photos. Have a video taken of yourself that demonstrates a skill, such as public speaking or teaching, then load it to YouTube. Post it to other sites where potential employers can see it as well.

Photos and videos aren't the only way to reveal your skills. Tailors or seamstresses can wear examples of the clothing they designed and sewed. An administrative assistant can offer a writing sample. A sales person might have a graph showing sales results. Staff members can present brochures, reports or newsletters as samples of their work. A mechanic can present pictures of auto restorations. Facilitators or trainers can use participant evaluations and videos of presentations. Other sources of work samples include hobbies, sports, scouts, hunting, fishing, crafts, volunteer work and other interests.

Work samples build self-confidence, prove your credibility and show your ability to finish tasks. Use them to illustrate your skills, abilities and accomplishments. After all, you're proud of what you've done and you should not feel apprehensive about showing it.

Despite the obvious advantages of having a portfolio, few employers see them during interviews. So how effective are they? Verizon Wireless "talent connector" Krystal Dominick says only three or four applicants out of the 300 interviews she conducts annually come in with a portfolio.

And how many people in that small group were hired? "All of them got jobs," she says. "The portfolios really help them showcase their experience and their job histories."

## Paper Portfolios

A portfolio is a method of organizing and presenting your skills that resonate with your occupational objective. An excellent way to illustrate your skills, your career, training and education, portfolios can help display your best work and provide you with a story to tell employers about your career and the challenges you overcame in various positions.

How do you start? For a paper portfolio, begin with a loose leaf binder with dividers. The first page can be a fresh copy of your resume, or you can place that in a pocket in the front cover. The content in the rest of the portfolio is best displayed in clear page protectors.

The first section of your portfolio should be used for your research on your target company. Go to the company's website to find information about it. There you can find "about us" statements, mission or value statements, and press releases. Even include a copy of an article that shows a challenge or problem a company's industry faces. Those articles can initiate a dialogue.

In the first section you could have a page that matches your skills with those sought by an employer if you are responding to a specific job opening notice. That will address quickly why you are a serious candidate for the job since your skill set will match the position, and the fact you went to the trouble of creating a portfolio will reveal your ambition and focus.

## CASE STUDY:

### MOLLY MCGINNIS

**A paralegal in search of** employment in a tough legal market, Molly McGinnis created a 43-page portfolio with separate sections such as "professional profile," "honors and awards," "paralegal skills," "computer skills" and "liberal arts."

Within those sections were subsections with a resume, letters of recommendation, awards, legal writing samples and Excel and PowerPoint examples, as well as a written essay from a college course she had taken. (See McGinnis' table of contents and "mission statement" in the Endnotes section of this chapter.)

The portfolio was not easy to put together, but it has paid off. "It took me two or three months to get it all together," says McGinnis. "But having a portfolio has really helped me in interviews. It gives me more of a professional appearance. Resumes basically tell interviewers, 'I did this, I did that,' but they can't know if what you're saying is true. With a portfolio you can show what you have done and what you can do."

How you organize the rest of the information in the portfolio is up to you. If your job requires working among different product categories or divisions, you can divide up the content in that way, with a handful of examples from each one. You could have partial samples of your output and offer full versions if the interviewer requests them. A 30-page PowerPoint in a portfolio is overkill, but a page or two would be fine. If the interviewer says, "I'd love to see the whole thing," email it later.

As the interview moves forward, refer back to the portfolio any time you can. Look for opportunities to show and tell the employer what you have done. Each time, pull out a copy to show the interviewer. Have a photocopy available to leave behind.

The content of the portfolio will be dictated by each person's experiences. For a list of potential items to put in a portfolio, go to page 92.

## E-Portfolios

E-portfolios such as Figdig.com or carbonmade.com are online compilations of what was just described in the previous section. You can use many of the same components in an e-portfolio, such as work samples, photographs, personal data, resumes, references, educational backgrounds, career objectives, volunteer activities, letters of recommendation, awards, badges and military records.

After creating a site, you can email a link to prospective employers, references, your network and anyone else who might have an interest. The pages are built to be clean and inviting, with a good, colorful template that allows for modification. Give it a test run to see if you can make it work for your career.

# PERSONAL WEBSITES

Online web creation sites such as About.me, Weebly, Google Sites or Wix, allow you to create a limited number of pages for free. You will pay for more pages through a monthly subscription. The free site, however, may be just enough to get your Web presence going.

What's good about websites and e-portfolios is that employers can see what you have done in a visual presentation that is not available in a written resume. If they like what they see on the resume and want to learn more about you, they can quickly skim your e-portfolio or website. The fact you developed an online presence will be impressive enough, and the work exhibited there should only help your cause. As in the past, make sure everything is spelled correctly, reads well and links to content work.

When you get to the interview, you can have the individual pull up the digital portfolio to assist in the discussion. With a paper or e-portfolio and/or a job website, you will have a nice assortment of informational sources describing your skills, career, values and volunteer pursuits. Having the website and e-portfolio will only strengthen your online presence in a positive way, a clear advantage when a potential employer decides to Google your name.

## POTENTIAL PORTFOLIO CONTENT DIVISIONS

- Employer/Industry Information (articles on the interviewer, employer and industry)
- Personal Information
- Project and Work Samples
- Skills List, Matched to Job
- Diplomas, Certifications, Transcripts, Special Licenses
- Workshops and Conferences
- References, Evaluations, Letters of Recommendation and Testimonials
- Awards
- Letters of Thanks
- Articles About You
- Stories Demonstrating Skills or Character (preferably signed)
- Writing Samples/Published Work
- Documentation/Photos of Speaking Events
- Presentations (computer, hard copy, etc.)
- Teamwork Examples
- "Before" and "After" Examples
- Leadership Examples
- Work Showing Computer Savvy, Such as Charts, Spreadsheets, Graphics, etc.
- Job Match Letter
- Questions for the Employer
- Note Pad

# E N D N O T E S :

| PERSONAL DATA RECORD | |
|---|---|
| Name | |
| Address | |
| Social Security Number | |
| Phone Numbers | Home                  Fax |
| Email | |

**Any Felony Convictions?** Yes ☐  No ☐  If yes, explain:

| | |
|---|---|
| Employment Desired | |
| Position Title | Starting Wage |
| Dates Available | |

| Available for Work (circle) | Full Time | Weekend | Part Time | On Call | Temporary | Seasonal | Rotating Shifts |
|---|---|---|---|---|---|---|---|

| EDUCATION | | | | | | |
|---|---|---|---|---|---|---|
| | High School | Business, Trade School, College | Undergraduate | College/ University | Graduate/ Professional | Military Training |
| School Name/GED® | | | | | | |
| School Location | | | | | | |
| Years Completed | Don't complete this information for high school— it either doesn't apply or could lead to age discrimination. | | | | | |
| Diploma/Degree | | | | | | |
| Graduation Date | | | | | | |
| Course of Study | | | | | | |
| Describe Any Scholastic Honors, Assistantships, Etc. | | | | | | |
| Describe Any Specialized Training, Assistantships, Etc. | | | | | | |
| Foreign Languages | | | | | | |
| Occupational License, Certifications, Registrations, Professional Affiliations | | | | | | |

<table>
<tr><td colspan="5">PERSONAL DATA RECORD (CONTINUED)<br>EMPLOYMENT HISTORY<br>(list most recent employment first)</td></tr>
<tr><td colspan="2">Employer Name/Organization</td><td colspan="3">Address</td></tr>
<tr><td colspan="2">Dates Employed—</td><td>From: Month/Year</td><td colspan="2">To: Month/Year</td></tr>
<tr><td colspan="2">Job Title/Major Responsibilities/Skills, Knowledge and Abilities</td><td colspan="3"></td></tr>
<tr><td colspan="2">Supervisor/ Leader</td><td>Contact?   Yes   No</td><td colspan="2">Phone</td></tr>
<tr><td colspan="2">Reason for Leaving</td><td colspan="3">Ending Salary</td></tr>
<tr><td colspan="2">Employer Name/Organization</td><td colspan="3">Address</td></tr>
<tr><td colspan="2">Dates Employed—</td><td>From: Month/Year</td><td colspan="2">To: Month/Year</td></tr>
<tr><td colspan="2">Job Title/Major Responsibilities/Skills, Knowledge and Abilities</td><td colspan="3"></td></tr>
<tr><td colspan="2">Supervisor/ Leader</td><td>Contact?   Yes   No</td><td colspan="2">Phone</td></tr>
<tr><td colspan="2">Reason for Leaving</td><td colspan="3">Ending Salary</td></tr>
<tr><td colspan="2">Employer Name/Organization</td><td colspan="3">Address</td></tr>
<tr><td colspan="2">Dates Employed—</td><td>From: Month/Year</td><td colspan="2">To: Month/Year</td></tr>
<tr><td colspan="2">Job Title/Major Responsibilities/Skills, Knowledge and Abilities</td><td colspan="3"></td></tr>
<tr><td colspan="2">Supervisor/ Leader</td><td>Contact?   Yes   No</td><td colspan="2">Phone</td></tr>
<tr><td colspan="2">Reason for Leaving</td><td colspan="3">Ending Salary</td></tr>
<tr><td colspan="5">VOLUNTEER ACTIVITY</td></tr>
<tr><td colspan="2">Dates Volunteered—</td><td>From: Month/Year</td><td colspan="2">To: Month/Year</td></tr>
<tr><td colspan="2">Title/Major Responsibilities/Skills, Knowledge and Abilities</td><td colspan="3"></td></tr>
<tr><td colspan="2">Supervisor/ Leader</td><td>Contact?   Yes   No</td><td colspan="2">Phone</td></tr>
<tr><td colspan="2">Other Skills, Knowledge and Abilities Not Listed Above Acquired Through Hobbies or Interests</td><td colspan="3"></td></tr>
</table>

---

## MOLLY MCGINNIS' MISSION STATEMENT AND PORTFOLIO TABLE OF CONTENTS

### Mission Statement

*To become a team member of success in a rewarding paralegal position with a quality law firm.*

*To utilize my experience, interest and skills in a dynamic law firm that offers challenges and professional development.*

### Table of Contents

**Professional Profile. . . . . . . . . . . . . Index pages 1-7**

- Mission Statement
- Resume
- Reference
- Letter of Recommendation

**Honors and Awards. . . . . . . . . . . Index pages 8-14**

- Academic Achievement
- Associate in Applied Science-Paralegal Certificate
- Associate in Applied Science-Medical Assistant Certificate

**Paralegal Skills . . . . . . . . . . . . . . Index pages 15-20**

- Legal Writing
- Legal Research
- Law Office Procedures and Technology
- Law Office Ethics

**Computer Skills . . . . . . . . . . . . . . Index pages 21-34**

- Ms Word
- Excel
- PowerPoint
- Access
- PC Law

**Liberal Arts . . . . . . . . . . . . . . . . Index pages 35-43**

- Writing Composition
- Essay Psychology

# CHAPTER 6

# How People Find Work

*"Find a job you like and you add five days to every week."*

— H. JACKSON BROWN JR., AUTHOR OF "LIFE'S LITTLE INSTRUCTION BOOK"

Today, companies are more selective in hiring employees due to a number of factors. They range from an overwhelming number of candidates to the economic climate, from employment legislation to new technologies, and from employer liability to organizational restructuring.

The average American will have many jobs and change careers many times during his or her lifetime. For some people — not all — a 21st century lesson of life is this: Get used to searching for a job. You are unlikely to stay at one employer, or even one career, your entire working life.

Employers seek job applicants by using a variety of approaches. We're going to take you through the most common methods. A later chapter will speak to the world of social media and how employers are using platforms such as LinkedIn and Facebook to find workers.

## HOW EMPLOYERS OPERATE

Understanding how employers hire — and where to find open positions in today's market — will help you tremendously in landing a job. You will need to consider and act upon ideas for impressing employers with your skills, background and knowledge. Knowing how employers think and presenting your best professional image to them is the key to success.

But it isn't easy. And the bottom line is that while you may "get" how employers hire new people, there will be times when you will be baffled, upset and mystified by the processes and outcomes.

Some employers may contact you with great interest and then not return your phone calls. You might get an interview and be assured of a position only to find the company had to pull back due to an acquisition, or the economy, or half a dozen other reasons that make sense or don't make sense.

On the good days you will discover a host of decent employers who like what you have to offer and sincerely want to speak to you. Ideally, you should roll with the punches. Prepare for potential setbacks but maintain a sense of optimism. The way you will feel when you get that new job will outweigh any setbacks incurred along the way.

## The Hiring Process

Larger employers have a formal hiring structure and often involve multiple people in the process. In contrast, smaller employers may have one individual assigned to handle the hiring, and the process may be less formal. Other issues arise. Industry-specific practices found in health care, education and government have unique hiring stages perhaps influenced by labor agreements.

Not everyone in a company has the authority to add new employees. Typically, a manager of the department where the person will work makes the final decision. When possible find out who makes the final decision. However, treat everyone as though they are the hiring authority during your encounters with potential employers. Kindness and curiosity will go a long way toward impressing employers and their staffs during the interviewing processes.

You will hear a lot about human resources departments. They manage the process, sometimes taking a first swipe at a pile of resumes and reducing their numbers by removing unqualified or under-qualified applicants. HR may be assigned to appointing entry-level applicants to positions, but the majority of its work involves recruiting, screening and scheduling interviews. Don't underestimate its influence when you're dealing with an employer.

Hiring practices vary based on particular industries, employers and hiring managers. Generally, however, employers follow a few common hiring strategies and tools to select candidates. It comes down to three stages: recruitment, screening and selection.

## Stage 1: Recruitment

Employers need an applicant pool to fill job openings. Employers who do extensive hiring may continuously recruit applicants even when they have no immediate need. The reason? To always have a deep pool of applicants. Employers who hire occasionally, or for very specialized positions, often recruit as needed. Others may be planning a future expansion and want to know if they could fill their labor needs. Actively recruiting does not always mean actual job openings.

Companies get the word out on jobs in a variety of ways, ranging from word of mouth, to advertising (on company websites and job boards, and in online and offline newspapers and trade publications), to hiring personnel staffing services to asking employees to refer qualified candidates to them.

## Stage 2: Screening

Once employers have an applicant pool, they narrow it down to the best qualified candidates. This comes after dozens, or hundreds, of applicants have been screened out of the pool. During the initial screening, employers usually spend no more than a few seconds on each application.

Larger companies often use applicant tracking systems to efficiently screen large applicant pools. Applicant tracking systems are designed to select candidates who have the desired qualifications for the job. The resume section in Chapter 4 addresses the need to consider those tracking systems when putting together your resume.

## Stage 3: Selection

Interviews are the key part of the hiring process. Companies use interviews to verify qualifications and to evaluate how you will fit into the organization. If you get a call for an interview, that means you passed one hurdle and are in the running for a position. It will be up to you to convince a company that you are the best qualified person for the job.

"Best qualified" can mean many things: skills, experience, education, motivation, a passion for excellence, and a dedication to continuous learning and quality. Companies want value for their money because every employee is a major expense in terms of salary and benefits. You have to convince an employer you are the best qualified.

# WHERE TO FIND JOBS

Finding job openings can seem fairly easy. Head for a huge job site like Monster.com, and it looks as though half the companies in the United States have openings. When you submit an application or resume you will find in many cases the competition numbers hundreds of people who also are using popular job websites. Still, an argument can be made that keeping an eye on those sites is not a bad idea since they will indicate which fields are growing and what companies are hiring.

Let's look at the most common sources of jobs and their pluses and minuses for job seekers.

## Advertised Jobs

Job openings can be found in trade journals, job boards, company websites, social networking services, newspapers, grocery stores, libraries and store windows. The most common of these are Internet job boards.

There are drawbacks to seeking advertised jobs. They often result in competition with hundreds of applicants. Not all jobs are advertised as companies move to posting jobs on their own websites and not on large job boards. Paul Sears, an employment counselor at the Minneapolis WorkForce Center, says he firmly believes WorkForce Center customers who crowd the computer terminals in his building's lobby "should spend more time on other job-hunting activities. I wish I could tell them to stop surfing the Web for jobs and start talking to people and networking. That's how you find a job."

Still, advertised jobs should not be overlooked. Here's a strategy for spending just enough but not too much time on positions listed in publications or on the Internet.

- Pick your sources for advertised jobs — specific Internet job boards, trade journals or newspapers. Review new listings when they're released.

- Don't waste time scanning several Internet job boards. Focus your efforts on one general job board and two or three niche sites specific to your industry or field.

- Respond to new openings immediately and don't bother responding to listings that run continuously or are old.

- Take caution when responding to blind ads, which require you to apply to an anonymous email address or P.O. Box. Do not apply to any jobs that don't appear to be from legitimate sources and never give out confidential information like Social Security or credit card numbers.

- Look at all the jobs listed, not just those that fit your goal, because you may find an employer you want to pursue. If they have an opening in one field, they may have one in your area of expertise, too, that isn't advertised.

- Follow up your application with a phone call to the employer.

## Networking

Employment experts agree that most job openings are never advertised. Only by knocking do doors open. Creative job searching demands a lot of calling, handshaking, chatting, explaining and conversing. Improving on your networking skills can help get you through the door to employers. The hidden job market, defined as positions that go unadvertised, cannot really be pursued by you without a strong effort at networking.

A formal networking campaign is a good idea, but try not to make the folks you meet feel as though you're using them in any way. Start by speaking to people you know well, such as friends, family, neighbors and former (or current) coworkers. These people have the most interest in your success and are excellent networking contacts. Now, contact people who pop up only occasionally in your life and career. More than 25 percent of the people who find jobs through networking received the referral from someone they see once a year or less. Ask this group for ideas and referrals, remind them of who you are and ask if they might be willing to meet for a 15-minute chat. Remember, honor that time limitation unless they insist on having you stay longer (a likely scenario since most people don't time conversations).

Next, join job seeking networking groups in your industry, city or congregation. Minnesota WorkForce Centers sponsor a host of networking groups around the state. You may get a tip

## TIPS FOR SUCCESSFUL NETWORKING CONVERSATIONS

- Keep the conversation focused.

- Relax. Networking conversations have specific goals, but that doesn't mean they can't be fun.

- Be curious and take an interest in the person you are networking with first.

- Be a journalist and ask lots of pertinent questions.

- Ask for help after having developed rapport. Speak of your career goals and ask if they have any advice, resources or tips to help you.

- Work hard to remember names, just like great politicians. When the person introduces herself, repeat her name back to her, as in: "It's a pleasure to meet you, Maria. My name is Joe."

- Ask for contact information. You'll need this to follow up.

- Keep your promises. If you offered to help someone else in a job search, always make good on your promises.

- Always follow up when you make a connection with a thank you note.

or two from other participants in the group, along with solace, advice, conversation and camaraderie.

Take those referrals and begin contacting them. These are the individuals you do not know, so you need to call and formally introduce yourself while highlighting the people who gave you their names. It's not an easy task and not everyone will call back or agree to meet. Still, these are the people who may have the responsibility for hiring or know the appropriate individual in their companies for you to contact.

Using social media websites will help you network, as well as build an online personal brand and search for jobs. See Chapter 7 for using social media for job hunting.

Finally, we suggest cold-calling. This is picking out companies where you would like to work and cold-calling managers or employees, asking them for informational interviews or ideas for finding a job where they work. They may avoid returning your call or tell you they have little to offer in the way of open positions. Still like that company? Try another division, or move down the list to the next prospective company in your sights.

It's a good idea to look at our "Networking Log" at the end of this chapter or develop your own template. Write down the people you contacted, their phone numbers and any leads they offered. If someone doesn't return your inquiry after a couple of calls, move on. Don't be a pest because that reputation could come back to haunt you.

Take notes during interviews, and afterward write an email and a personal handwritten thank you to people who took the time to speak to you. Do not overstay your welcome, and focus on getting the information you require in an informational interview. Always ask for more contacts, too, to broaden your list.

Networking is not begging. The idea is not to ask for jobs but to ask for information that may lead to a job. Usually your networking contacts will not be potential employers. They will be people who know about potential jobs or individuals in an industry who can help. If you discover contacts are potential employers with job openings that fit your skills, change gears and begin to sell yourself.

## Career Fairs

Many different organizations have career fairs featuring employers willing to speak to potential employees. Ideally, job seekers have a chance to actually meet company or college representatives who can help them find employment or introduce them to new careers.

It's a great networking opportunity because job seekers have a chance to speak directly to employers. And in a perfect world, those employers have jobs to offer.

Career fairs can be a mixed experience. Attend them with the hope of making a few connections. You may find them worth your time or you may find your efforts are better spent pursuing other avenues of employment.

# TIPS FOR MAKING THE MOST OF CAREER FAIRS

### Choose a Career Fair

- You can learn about a wide range of career fairs across Minnesota at http://mn.gov/deed/. The day, time and location of events are listed with links for more details.

- Select events to add to your calendar and receive reminder emails or text messages.

- If you don't live in Minnesota, check out http://jobcenter.usa.gov. The site allows you to find the job center closest to you, so you can connect with job search resources in your area.

### Before the Career Fair

- Develop and practice a one-minute self-marketing introduction, including a greeting, your expertise, accomplishments and areas of interest. Start a conversation. Don't give an advertisement.

- Research companies participating in the career fair.

- Prepare questions that show interest and knowledge about the organizations.

- Arrange for others to take care of family responsibilities, such as daycare, while you will be attending.

### During the Career Fair

- Go alone, or if you go with others, walk the career fair floor by yourself.

- Be professional. Use your self-marketing introduction, demonstrating interest and enthusiasm.

- Dress as you would for a job interview.

- Ask relevant questions and answer questions clearly and concisely, showing the knowledge you acquired about the company.

- Collect company information, request a business card, take notes and ask about follow-up procedures.

- Repeat your interest in the company, offer a resume and thank employers for their time.

- Attend workshops for job seekers and participate in resume critiques where offered.

### After the Career Fair

- Send a thank you letter within three days of the career fair.

- Contact the employer afterward to remind him or her of your continued interest in employment opportunities, preferably with a phone call. If you don't receive a response, call again.

## MAKING CONTACT WITH EMPLOYERS

The goal of any job search campaign is to meet face-to-face with employers in an interview. The more interviews you have, the greater your chances for success. Most job seekers, however, prefer a passive job search strategy in which they submit an application or resume and wait. When they don't hear anything they start all over again by answering another ad or contacting a company only through email or regular mail.

Instead of those passive attempts at getting a job, try a more active approach by taking initiative and making direct contact with potential employers.

Direct employer contact requires preparation, confidence and persistence. Many people are uncomfortable with this tactic, afraid of offending the employers with too much aggressiveness. Yet going straight to an employer works, even if you already answered an advertised job. Showing a strong desire to work for a company without becoming too bothersome — a fine line to tread — will likely yield success faster than answering online ads.

### LOOKING IN YOUR BACKYARD

Having been let go by a major hotel chain due to a decline in business, Lisa Stallman figured her next job would likely be in something other than the hit-hard-by-the-recession hospitality industry.

In looking for a new job, Stallman, a two-decade veteran of hotel management, had the goal of staying close to home in the vicinity of Brooklyn Park, Minn., and the northwest Twin Cities suburbs in order to be close to her children and husband.

One day while traveling down Wyoming Avenue and 93rd Street she pulled over into a parking lot of an office park, took out of her wallet a store receipt and began writing on the back of it the names of businesses at that location.

Then, Stallman went home and began to research those companies to see if they had openings. She looked into firms in fitness, book publishing and convention exhibits before calling Coffee Mill Inc., a company providing hot and cold beverages to offices in the Twin Cities region.

The owner of the family-operated business spoke to Stallman several times before hiring her within a span of just two weeks. As a "sales associate," Stallman has a chance to use her hospitality training and connections to win clients.

The search may have been unconventional, but it worked. "It was a matter of going out and meeting my neighbors — both businesses and people in our neighborhood — and letting them know I was looking for a job," she says. "It's great to be able to find one good opportunity not far from my front door."

Richard Bolles, the celebrated author of "What Color is Your Parachute?" says that using his creative approach to finding a job is most effective. The difference from a traditional approach, in which you post your resume online, look for vacancies and approach companies via your resume, lies in how you go about identifying which organizations to approach. Using his creative approach, you do a careful inventory of yourself to decide what organizations match you. Then you approach them, this time through a person, specifically a bridge person — someone who knows them and also knows you.

Bolles cites research that looked at the different methods of finding an opening, such as answering ads or using private employment agencies. Bolles reports that:

- His creative approach works 86 percent of the time. You have a 12 times better chance of finding work using this method than if you just sent out your resume.

- Using the Yellow Pages works 65 percent of the time. It involves going through the Yellow Pages of your local phone book or the Index to those Yellow Pages, so you can identify subjects or fields of interest to you. Then you go from the Index to the actual Yellow Pages and look up names of organizations and companies in those fields, in that town or city where you want to work. You call them, set up an appointment, go visit them, and explore whether or not they are hiring for the kind of work you do, or the position you are looking for. It's a lot harder to get employers (at large companies anyway) to consent to see you these days. But you have a nine times better chance of finding a job with this method, than if you just depended on your resume.

- Knocking on the door of any employer, office, or manufacturing plant works 47 percent of the time.

- Job-search support groups have a job-hunting success rate that is usually around 10 percent (if that.) However, there are some rare exceptions, with a much higher success rate of 50 percent.

## BASIC PRINCIPLES OF DIRECT EMPLOYER CONTACT

Networking and research will land you plenty of names of companies and individuals within them as contacts while pursuing a job.

Are you ready to contact employers directly? Good, because it works. Now, let's look at effective ways to do it.

Start with contacting employers by phone. When you make direct contact, don't begin by asking if they're hiring or by saying you're unemployed.

Avoid being transferred to the human resources department unless you have been told it is the hiring authority. If you hear you should submit an application or resume, ask if you can have an informational interview either by phone or in person. Tell the individuals with whom you speak that you're less interested in simply submitting a resume and more interested in learning about the company. Should you receive a brush off and request to submit online or mail the resume, kindly say you will abide by the company's process and that you will stay in touch following your submission of job-related materials.

Whenever possible, make the next step your responsibility — not the employer's. For example, if an employer says, "We will call you in a couple of weeks," you could respond with,

"Would it be all right if I call you two weeks from today?" If they say, "Yes," then you've agreed on your follow-up, and the responsibility is yours.

When you contact an employer, you might reach a receptionist before speaking with a manager or executive. Think of receptionists and other "gatekeepers" as the eyes and ears of decision makers. Receptionists tend to put in a good word for people who treat them with courtesy and respect.

Should you get an informational interview, conduct research on the company prior to your appointment. We have plenty of details on researching companies elsewhere in this book, and we suggest you take a look at it. And expect rejection. It goes with the territory. Don't take it personally. Maintain a good attitude and a healthy sense of humor.

### Telephoning Tips

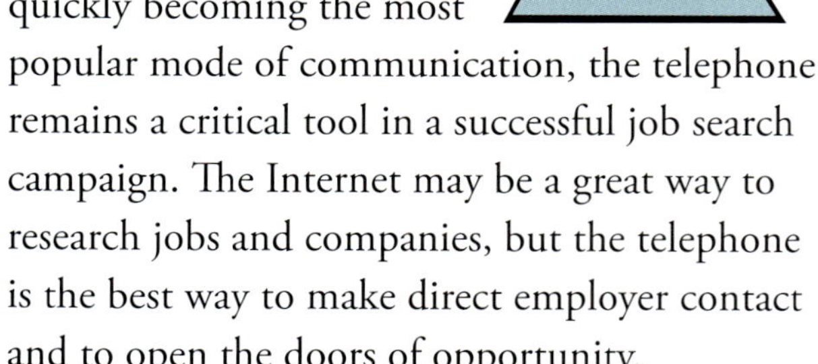

Although the Internet is quickly becoming the most popular mode of communication, the telephone remains a critical tool in a successful job search campaign. The Internet may be a great way to research jobs and companies, but the telephone is the best way to make direct employer contact and to open the doors of opportunity.

Effective telephone techniques are critical skills all job seekers need, and they can be learned. You need to learn how to script a call, the basics of sounding competent on a phone and the importance of having a follow-up strategy that appeals to employers.

Some people have a hard time with the idea of selling their qualifications over the phone. Nobody wants to sound pushy or unprepared, but learning how to sell yourself is critical to a successful job search.

Just like a sales call, you will get about 20 seconds to capture the employer's attention. Therefore, communication has to be to the point and concise. Even the best communicators use scripting to make sure they get their point across. It helps to relieve jitters and keep the conversation focused.

Have an objective for the call. You may be seeking information, trying to schedule a meeting or presenting your qualifications to a potential employer. Have a secondary objective. Often you won't achieve your primary objective, but every telephone call is an opportunity to seek information.

Make a call to get the name of the person you want to speak to and then either have the receptionist transfer you or redial and make a direct call to that individual.

Outline in writing what you want to say. This is important in the early stages of cold-calling or when the call is important. Later on, you'll script most of your calls in your head. Don't read your script. Your presentation should be natural.

## A MODEL TELEPHONE SCRIPT

**Caller:** Hi. This is Jerry Job. I'm trying to contact the person in charge of marketing. Who would that be?

**Receiver:** That's Lisa Ramirez. She is the director.

**Caller:** I would like to contact her. Does she have a direct number or an extension number?

**Receiver:** Her direct number is 555-555-5555. Would you like me to transfer you?

**Caller:** Please do.

## A MODEL FOLLOW-UP SCRIPT

**Caller:** Hello. This is Jerry Job. I interviewed for the computer programmer position last week. I'm just checking to see if the hiring decision has been made.

**Receiver:** Not yet. We anticipate making our final selection this Wednesday.

**Caller:** I'm still very interested in the position. You're doing some very innovative multimedia work that's cutting edge. You have a bright and energetic technical staff and working with them really appeals to me. Would it be OK if I called you on Wednesday? What's a good time?

The script will depend on the goal of the call and whether you know the person you are calling. A good script should include an introduction that describes who you are and whether you were referred. State the purpose of your call and then ask for information or to schedule the meeting.

---

## PHONE SKILLS 101

- Practice your skills on a spouse or friend. Tape yourself to hear how you sound.

- Deal with voice mail. Leave your name and phone number (twice, and slowly) and the reason for the call. Be upbeat, simple, clear and concise. Avoid the monotone. If you are offered the option to review your message, do so just to check it.

- If you have an answering machine, make sure your message is polite and professional. It's not cute or clever, by the way, to have your children do the message on a phone line that will be used by potential employers.

- Organize all your job search materials nearby and take notes.

- Listen carefully. If you sense you've called at a bad time, politely ask if there's a better time. Listen for "buy" signals, among them questions about qualifications or about other topics. They're showing an interest in you.

- Handle objections such as "We're looking for someone with more experience or education" or "Sorry, we're not hiring right now" with a response that continues to sell your qualifications.

- Follow up: The persistent 20 percent make 80 percent of the sales. While you have the contact on the telephone, agree on when you'll call back. Keep a follow-up calendar and maintain a record of your contacts. If someone agrees to call you, give a time you can be reached — or your mobile phone number.

- Stand up during cold calls. Being erect will improve your posture and expand your lungs, making you sound more alert.

- If you can't get past the receptionist, try before 8 a.m., during lunch, after 5 p.m. or Saturday morning. If you still can't get through, solicit the receptionist's assistance.

- Look for ways to compliment the person or the company. Sell your strengths, skills and accomplishments.

## Emailing Tips

Email is the easiest way to apply for a job opening and the easiest inquiry for employers to avoid. If you catch a manager on the phone you can try to make a quick pitch. You may hear a grunt and a "Sorry, we're not hiring" or a "Hey, why don't you come in. Let's set up a time." Managers are usually overwhelmed with internal and external emails daily, so trying to capture their attention can be difficult.

A more creative strategy combines email, calling and mailing managers your information. Call it the one-two digital/verbal punch.

The approach is to email the prospect a short letter of just a paragraph saying you're interested in an advertised job or you're wondering if any positions are currently open. Stress that you will call within a day or two. Skip writing a long cover letter — unless an advertised job has been posted — because effective emails tend to be brief. In a case of an available opening, many employers recommend making the email message the cover letter.

Attach your resume, written in Word or as an Adobe PDF document, to email correspondence related to finding a job. Managers can open either format with little problem. Then call within a day or two and, if leaving a message, remind the individual of the day and time you sent the email and attachment and spell your name. Email

programs can segment messages by day, time, subject line and sender. The person can locate it faster with the information you just provided.

Then print out and send via U.S. mail what you emailed. This illustrates your high level of interest in the position and the company, and your commitment to making certain the manager and others at the firm see your resume.

# COUNSELING AND STAFFING SERVICES

Personnel staffing services and contract firms can be excellent job search resources. Organized as private or nonprofit public entities, they specialize in service to specific groups of companies and employment clients. For example, a common field such as information technology will be the focus of dozens of contract firms in a large metropolitan area. A smaller number of staffing firms may work specifically to assist people with disabilities in finding jobs.

Each firm is unique and may provide a combination of blended services. The type of services offered may be influenced by whom they represent: you or the employer. Generally, their focus is on matching your skills with the job openings of employers or companies. Depending on your circumstances and needs, these outsourcing companies benefit you in securing employment. They fall into several categories.

*Staffing/Recruiting*: Employers use staffing services to assist them in filling their job openings. Staffing agencies recruit, perform extensive interviewing, check references and submit only the most qualified applicants to the employer. Some staffing services offer a bulletin board service where job orders and/or resumes are posted and job seekers and employers interact without any agency interference.

*Job Search Training*: Minnesota WorkForce Centers and other job centers around the country, as well as staffing services, offer specific training in job search skills to enable you to successfully find your own job. To locate a facility near you, try (http://jobcenter.usa.gov) or (www.servicelocator.org). This training may include individual workshops and materials on a variety of job search topics. Classes, which usually are free, focus on skills identification, resume writing and interviewing. If offered by private companies a fee will be charged.

*Career Counseling and Planning*: If you're looking for a job or entering the labor market for the first time, consider talking with a career counselor to help you with self-assessment, knowledge of the labor market, employment trends and training opportunities. These companies offer aptitude, interest, personality and skills testing to help you with career changes and to fulfill your potential by matching you to employment opportunities.

*Outplacement or Career Transition*: When companies downsize their workforces, some firms provide laid-off employees with outplacement assistance such as job search workshops and materials, phone rooms, job leads, resume design, a job club and employment counseling. Ask your employer if these services will be provided.

*Temporary and Contract Employment*: These firms refer you to temporary employment opportunities as requested by an employer who specifies the job requirements and time period of the work assignment. You work for the temporary or contract firm during this time and they pay you. By performing well you may get a full-time offer after your contract ends. Some positions, however, fill only short-term or seasonal needs, such as during the holiday rush or in summer.

## Benefits of Being a Contract Worker

Of the personnel service arrangements available, being a contract or temporary employee is the most advantageous. By working in contract jobs you can build skills and meet financial needs while continuing to look for permanent work. It's easier to get a job when you have a job. You might get more flexible hours or working conditions to accommodate your personal situation as well as help with transportation, testing, training, child care and health care.

This type of employment can also be useful for those who need to gain work experience, develop skills, get training or increase networking contacts. It's also a good way to check out an employer or an occupation before making a commitment to training, a career path or a particular employer. Personnel staffing services that offer temporary or contract employment provide a variety of services and options for the job seeker, but keep in mind the following considerations:

- Check into the firm's reputation. Determine if any fees will be charged for services before accepting or signing anything.

- These type of firms work with the job market daily and can provide valuable information that's helpful in your job search. Treat them as you'd treat a potential employer because they can expose you to many opportunities that are otherwise not available.

- If you're working with a contract or temporary staffing service, don't assume you can sit back and wait for jobs. Continue your search.

- Temporary firms are your employers when you're on assignment for them. Ask about items you need to know before you agree to accept employment. You need to know the pay rate, benefits, estimated length of assignment, the chance of becoming an employee of the company and what's expected of you. Also, let them know the hours and days you're available, your overtime availability, and your transportation and salary needs.

- Consider the secondary objectives of the service. An example might be career counseling provided by training or educational institutions. They may have a primary interest in enrolling you in their training program for funding reasons.

- Check out their placement rates and services with the Department of Education, Better Business Bureau or with former students.

- If you're receiving unemployment insurance benefits, you should realize short-term wages may affect eligibility and benefit amounts.

# E N D N O T E S :

## NETWORKING LOG

*It's important to document and follow up on all job leads. Use this sheet for keeping track of all your networking activity. Always ask your contacts to suggest other contacts. Keep at it.*

| | |
|---|---|
| **Employer Name** | |
| **Contact Name** | |
| **Address** | |
| **Email** | |
| **Fax** | |
| **Website** | |
| **Action Plan** | |
| **Appointment Date/Time** | |
| **Follow up** | |
| **Summary of Conversation/ Contact** | |
| **Additional Contacts Received** | |

# NOTES

# CHAPTER 7

# Using the Internet and Social Media

*" …The more people can "see" you on Facebook, Twitter, Google+, or a blog, the more they will feel like they know you, even though you don't have one-on-one interaction with them."*

— THOM S. RAINER

Having a positive, consistent presence on social media sites makes it easier for hiring managers to find you. And if you don't have an online presence, you run the risk of looking obsolete to recruiters.

Many job counselors warn that the Internet can be a giant swamp where you can apply repeatedly to no avail. And the numbers show that the percentages of online job applications that result in job interviews are few, according to Dr. John Sullivan in "Why You Can't Get A Job … Recruiting Explained By the Numbers." Here's what he says: For the specific case of an online job posting, on average, 1,000 individuals will see a job post, 200 will begin the application process, 100 will complete the application, 75 of those 100 resumes will be screened out by either the Applicant Tracking System or a recruiter, 25 resumes will be seen by the hiring manager and 4 to 6 will be invited for an interview.

But that doesn't mean you shouldn't apply for jobs online. Spend a few minutes a day tracking openings in your field and your area, but not a few hours. It's quality over quantity. Apply for jobs that you are a great fit for, not just an OK fit. When job hunting on the Internet, focus is important. In a hyperlinked universe, it's too easy to be distracted and link to site after site on unrelated subjects, avoiding the goal of finding a job. Stay the course. If you lose track, log off.

## JOB HUNTING ONLINE

Here are some tools you can employ to keep your browsing to a minimum and your networking and information gathering to a maximum.

### Company Websites

Many companies list their job openings primarily on their corporate websites, a practice that saves them money and keeps the job pool, to a degree, filled by people interested in working there. A posting on a company's website that does not appear on public job boards is appealing to job seekers. Remember though some aggregators simply pull those openings off corporate websites, opening them to a broader audience.

A company's website is the first place to go when researching specific employers. You may often find vision and mission statements, a history of the organization and names of key supervisors. Large companies typically require job seekers to use their website's online application to be considered for all of their openings.

## Employment Websites

These sites, sometimes called "job boards," are among the most popular ways to find job leads on the Internet. You can use keywords to find jobs based on certain criteria. They help you get more specific results by location, field, industry or job title. One of the most common mistakes that job seekers make is spending too many hours browsing job boards.

Job expert Peter Weddles came up with a strategy for using job boards that goes like this: 2GP+3N=1GJ. (2GP stands for two general-purpose websites; 3N for three niche or specialized sites and 1GJ for one great job.) General job boards list thousands of jobs from thousands of employers, the drawback being the popularity of these sites can be a disadvantage. For this reason, dedicate more of your attention to niche job boards focusing on openings in specific industries.

## Online Periodicals

The Internet is the fastest way to access published information. Newspapers, magazines and trade journals can all be found online. Trade journals contain articles by industry experts, information about networking events, suggestions on industry blogs and jobs. To find a trade journal related to your search, try typing "trade journal directory" into a search engine. Or, go to your public library for help accessing trade journal and professional association databases.

## Association Websites

Almost every industry has an association with a website full of information on trends, volunteer or professional development opportunities, best practices, industry news and, inevitably, a job board. It may require membership in the organization to get at the really good content and the job board. Most charge annual fees so you'll have to determine whether the fee is worth it.

## TIPS FOR INTERNET JOB SEARCHES

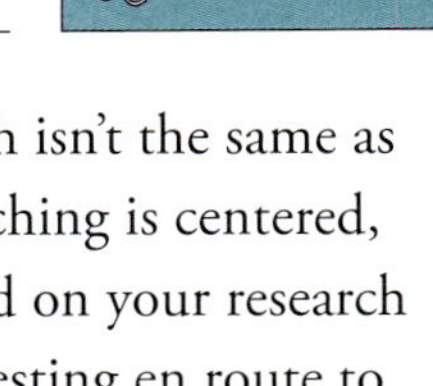

Using the Internet for research isn't the same as surfing the Internet. Researching is centered, surfing is wandering. Stay focused on your research goal. If you find something interesting en route to your goal, bookmark the site and come back to it. Here are some tips to keep you from getting lost in the mire of the Web.

## Develop a Research Strategy

Develop a plan before you begin looking for information. Decide in advance how much time you're willing to invest. Your topic will influence where you look. Knowing roughly where your information might be found will help in developing your plan. Remember, "Plan your work, then work your plan."

## Keep Records

It's important to keep a record of your research. As you explore potential employers, industries and communities, you will collect a lot of information. Discard anything that has little or no immediate value, then file and maintain information that you want to keep. Don't give in to the temptation to bookmark sites without discretion. The result is almost always an unmanageable tangle.

## Set Goals

Stay on track and have a goal. "I'm going to spend the next hour researching two potential employers who might need someone with marketing skills" is far better stated than "I'm going to look for jobs on the Internet."

## Posting Your Resume Online

Many employers manage and sort resumes in a resume database. They search the database for specific skills, experience and qualifications, so a well-written resume with the right skills, experience and qualifications will show up frequently and prominently in the employer's search. One advantage is that your resume is more easily found in the database. If the resume doesn't show up in a search today, it has a chance of showing up in a search in the future.

## CASE STUDY:

### A MINNESOTAN FINDS WORK THE NEW FASHION WAY

**Rachel Pinneg is member of a** new generation of job seekers who communicate with friends and learn of open positions through social networks.

While a graduate student in library science at the University of St. Catherine in St. Paul, Pinneg began using PB Works, a collaboration platform. She liked it so much she asked the Silicon Valley company if it had any needs for a part-time employee, one who happened to live in St. Paul.

The company liked her resume and agreed to work out an arrangement. Then Pinneg's husband, Matt, got a job at Apple. The couple moved to the Bay Area and PB Works asked Pinneg to work full time.

Eventually, she managed 12 people at PB Works, but she was restless. Pinneg set up a few RSS feeds, which are automated services that alert subscribers when their favorite sites have been updated. After setting an RSS feed on Craigslist, she learned of another job at a startup called Syncplicity.

Now, she's at Syncplicity. "Everyone pretty much uses social media out here," says Pinneg, 26. "It's all very networking based, whether it's through Facebook, or Twitter, or networking events. Social media is just another way to network."

There are several common ways that a resume is placed into a database. It may be entered directly to a job board or at an employer's website. Many sites allow you to upload resumes in standard formats such as Word or as a PDF. Pay attention to the directions on the website for uploading resumes and cover letters; a good first impression for a potential employee is the ability to follow directions.

## SOCIAL MEDIA SERVICES

*"Any social media platform is worth examining. Social media expands business, develops relationships, product innovation and service delivery – what an incredibly powerful communication tool."*

--TOBY DAYTON, PRESIDENT AND CEO, LINKUP.COM

Career experts agree — job seekers should use social media. LinkedIn, Twitter and Facebook are among the most popular social media websites for job hunting. Access them on your computer, or through their apps for tablets and smartphones.

Social media sites continue to evolve. Some that are popular today may be replaced by new technologies in the future. Since social media sites are playing an increasing role in job hunting, job seekers need to keep up with the latest technologies. Your local WorkForce Center can help you stay current.

LinkedIn has emerged as the most popular networking tool for professional and business purposes. Recruiters say this is a top choice to find workers because the candidate pool includes "passive" job seekers as well as job applicants. In addition, LinkedIn launched University Pages to help high school students look at colleges. The idea is to expand a student's understanding of the careers available, and get a head start on building a network of family and friends to help guide them along the way.

Facebook and Twitter, two of the most popular social networking tools, primarily started out as a way for people to communicate with friends and acquaintances. That has changed ... a lot.

In general, social networking services first ask you to create a profile that has information about your interests and activities, career and education. Once you complete your profile, you can search for people you know. You can request that certain friends and acquaintances become a part of your network, and they can accept or reject the offer.

Post meaningful tidbits from your life or job search. Skip useless information about what you ate today or anything that doesn't add value to your job search. Include links to photographs, articles, videos and other content related to your career or personal interests. These are far more valuable to your social network.

Connecting through the Internet may relieve some of the stress of traditional face-to-face networking because it can be easier to communicate through a typed message than to call someone you don't know very well. When you meet people ask which social media they use and if you could connect with them that way, too.

Social networks also offer a way for you to build your personal brand, a strategy discussed in Chapter 3. By having accounts on major social media sites you can build an image for yourself as an expert in a field and an intriguing personality.

Keep your image on social networking sites professional. Some studies show as many as 80 percent of employers look at your social networking profiles to see how you act beyond the interview.

Now let's take a look at these three popular social media sites.

## LinkedIn

LinkedIn is a social networking site specifically for connecting with other business and individuals. It will be key to your social networking strategy because it helps you establish connections with coworkers at past jobs, former managers, and your network of friends and acquaintances. Founded in 2002 and launched in May 2003, LinkedIn now counts more than 200 million members as part of its network, with representation in more than 200 countries and territories.

The network provides an important user base for job seekers. According to online marketer Lewis Howes, 45 percent of business professionals on LinkedIn are business decision makers.

Job seekers can establish a professional presence online by creating a resume, gaining recommendations and answering questions. There is also a job board that allows groups and businesses to post openings. The most important item to remember about LinkedIn is that simply creating a profile will not help you make the connections to find a job. You must interact and create valuable content and connections to resonate with employers and other members alike. For free webinars to help you learn to use LinkedIn, visit http://learn.linkedin.com/job-seekers/.

Use LinkedIn to remind your network contacts of your availability for employment and to share with them your insights on industries or events or information on business issues. Those members, in turn, can link you to members you may not know but who could have job openings at their companies or be aware of openings elsewhere. Join LinkedIn alumni, special interest and industry groups, list your skills that will get you endorsements, and participate in group discussions. Groups sometimes discuss various job openings. Having connections won't get you the position, but joining groups and offering meaningful answers to questions will call attention to your expertise and showcase your value.

## Twitter

This micro-blogging social media platform allows members to follow one another and send messages no longer than 140 characters, or around two sentences. Politicians promote their ideas to constituents, news organizations give information about stories as they develop, celebrities keep fans updated on their lives, and regular folks reveal, well, anything they want, from their passions to what's up with their kids. A message is called a tweet. By linking a message to a longer article, video or photo gallery, users add more value to their tweet.

These short messages provide a perfect electronic platform to let people know you are looking for a job — and to establish yourself as a valuable candidate for the jobs you seek. You could use Twitter to refer your followers to your LinkedIn page, to inform them you recently graduated from a college, or to tweet about things going on in your career. You can impress employers and people in your network by linking to articles or grabbing relevant quotes on your industry. If you want to tweet a link to something, but the URL consumes most of your 140-character limit, use www.tinyurl.com to shorten the length.

And don't forget to use Twitter's search capabilities: Search by job or industry hashtags for jobs on Twitter and do advanced searches. Visit other websites for finding jobs on Twitter such as TweetMyJobs.com or Tweetdeck.com.

In "Twitter Helped Me Get a New Job: 5 Success Stories," by Amy Levin-Epstein on CBS MoneyWatch, UCLA graduate Jessica Humphrey shared how she found employment:

Looking for a job in PR, Humphrey started following the Bread & Butter Public Relations Twitter account and soon found they were looking for interns. After interviewing, the company offered her an internship but she "needed to pay the bills" and declined. Still, she kept in contact with the company's team in Austin and saw tweets about an opening in its new San Francisco office. She received great recommendations from the company's Austin team and landed the job.

## Facebook

Facebook is by far the largest social media platform. Facebook connects friends and colleagues and provides spaces for conversations, videos, photographs and, of course, profiles of users. It has apps for job search such as Jobvite, which lets people connect and apply to jobs all within Facebook, and gives you the option to join Facebook Groups to find jobs in your field.

Facebook's Advanced Search function can be useful when job hunting. Use it to find profiles of people who attended a certain college, who once worked at a particular company or who live in your community. You can even search for people by location, age and first name — in case you've forgotten their surnames.

In an effort to get to know their job applicants, employers often look at Facebook accounts of applicants. According to a survey of more than 300 hiring professionals, a whopping 69 percent of recruiters have rejected a candidate based on content found on his or her social networking profiles — an almost equal proportion of recruiters (68 percent), though, have hired a candidate based on his or her presence on those networks. Post only comments and images on Facebook and other social media sites that you would want your prospective boss to see and adjust your privacy settings appropriately.

## OTHER SOCIAL MEDIA WEBSITES

LinkedIn, Twitter and Facebook are top social media sites used by job seekers. But, there are other social media websites you can also use for job hunting, including Google+, YouTube and Pinterest. YouTube can be used to promote yourself to employers via videos. Google+ works a lot like Facebook, and Pinterest, similar to an online corkboard, lets you easily integrate photos and other images into your job search tool kit.

## Blogs

Short for weblog, blogs are used by individuals, professionals, businesses and corporations. Usually a more professional blog will have a specific focus, such as landscaping, architecture, engineering or fashion. Blogs offer authors a forum to share their knowledge, thoughts or ideas. Posts are short pieces, generally, although some can go long when the topic demands it. Posts feature photos, videos and text, and a place where visitors can interact by sending an email or a video.

A series of posts about the same subject is called a "thread." You can join a conversation by commenting on a post or simply read what people are saying. Keep comments professional and related to the subject. Diverting from the subject or leaving inappropriate comments is considered poor "netiquette."

Create and use your own blog to reflect your expertise in your career field and to reinforce your personal brand. Speak about industry trends or highlight white papers, articles and other content you have produced regarding your profession, and remember to link them to your Facebook and Twitter accounts. Popular free websites for bloggers are WordPress, TypePad and Blogger. As with all social media, users should be careful about what they say, how they say it, and how much information they disclose.

Some people have lost their jobs or been passed over by a potential employer because of comments they've made in blog posts.

In terms of your job search, reading blogs is an effective way to get an "insider look" at various occupations, industries or fields. Reading a specific company's blog is a great way to expand your research. When interviewing, it is important to show that you are up-to-date on the happenings in your field of interest. Since many blogs are written by experts — self-proclaimed or otherwise — keep an eye out for good ones that will give you great insights into trends in your profession.

## JOB BLOGS

www.Blog.MinnesotaWorks.net

www.mnheadhunter.com

http://blog.simplyhired.com/

http://iseekinteractive.org/blog/

http://eblogger.com

# NOTES

# CHAPTER 8

# Facing Unemployment at 50 and Older

*"The other day a man asked me what I thought was the best time of life. 'Why,' I answered without a thought, 'now.'"*

— DAVID GRAYSON, AMERICAN JOURNALIST

Over 50 is far from over the hill. Some employers may quietly view older workers as technologically challenged, skeptical of the unknown and expensive. Of course, all of these attributes can be seen in younger workers as well, but they seem to be applied more often to workers beyond even 40 years old. Age discrimination is an issue that is growing louder as baby boomers move into their 50s and face obstacles they once thought were only reserved for their parents.

A 2013 AARP survey found that nearly one in five workers ages 45 to 74 believed that they hadn't gotten hired as a result of their age. Also, the survey found that over one-third reported that they or someone they know has experienced age discrimination. Even the federal Age Discrimination in Employment Act (ADEA) can't deny the reality that some employers consciously or subconsciously avoid hiring older workers.

Bob Skladany, an online columnist for the AARP.org website, notes: "While the ADEA makes age-based discrimination in hiring, pay, benefits, training, advancement and termination illegal, many people over 50, and increasingly older than 40, believe that age bias still exists and affects them."

But don't get discouraged. The website Go60.com says older workers get new jobs at an annual rate of 4.1 percent — more than double the rate of the general population — and account for 22 percent of the nation's job growth despite being only 10 percent of its workforce. By 2016 the number of employees 55 and older will rise by nearly 50 percent to more than 37 million.

The best approach to finding a job at any age is to face it head on and make changes as needed. The proverb "you're only as old as you feel" is applicable in job hunting; you want to recapture the energy of your youth and mix it with the toughness and experience of age. And you may want to adopt slightly different tactics from those used by younger workers in dealing with research, resumes and interviewing.

## Research

Applying everywhere probably isn't going to work, if it ever did. Whenever you're networking or speaking to friends, family and acquaintances, ask if they know anyone in a position to hire, or more specifically, any employers who prefer hiring older workers. Networking is how most people find employment; older job seekers tend to know more people who have been working or are working than younger job seekers, which is a distinct advantage. In your community, it is likely that most companies care less about age and more about quality of work. Try to find out who they are and then begin making contacts.

There are several online resources available for older job seekers such as the AARP website, RetiredBrains.com, seniorjobbank.com, workforce50.com and CareerBuilder.com (Advice & Resources). Retirementjobs.com lists jobs and offers "Age Friendly Certification" to employers that are open to hiring older workers.

## Resumes

Older workers who have had many positions and years of work could obviously fill up many pages of a  resume. The temptation is to showcase your entire career to make the point that no one else applying has been in the trenches as long as you. Avoid this strategy at all costs.

A resume is not a history. It's a tactical, "living" tool to showcase how your skills and accomplishments make you the top candidate for the position/occupation you're applying for today.

Older workers should limit and focus their experience depending on what they are applying for. If it's a managerial job, go back 15 years; a technical job, 10 years; and a high-tech job, three years. You might place older jobs into the "Other Experience" category or eliminate them altogether.

When writing your resume, it's OK to leave a few things out, especially irrelevant jobs you held in the distant past. List where you went to school and your degrees, not the years you received them. Emphasize your flexibility in the cover letter and on the resume. After all, you've spent "a few years" managing and adjusting to change.

Other key points to get across in the resume or cover letter: (1) your desire for a long-term position, (2) your solid attendance history, (3) your reliability and honesty, (4) your flexibility, (5) your ability to learn new skills, and (6) training and professional development courses and programs you have attended.

Computer skills are important in nearly all positions these days. Some employers may assume folks in mid-career lack these skills, so it's your job to dispel this myth early and clearly. List your computer software and technology-related skills as close to the top of Page 1 of your resume as possible. Go ahead and set up free

LinkedIn, Twitter or other social media accounts and include these, along with your email address, in your contact information at the top of Page 1.

If your resume is several years old, there is a good chance it needs a new format. Update your template! Remember to save it as both a plain text file (RTF) for uploading to websites and as a Word file for physical distribution through the mail, or as an attachment.

Show you're up to date! Make sure the words in your resume reflect terminology that is currently used in your field. If you're uncertain about current  terminology, you could do some research by reading industry publications, checking out association websites and, if you're not a member, joining a professional group.

The whole focus of an older worker's resume should be on matching skills and accomplishments with the open position, not a recap of a long career.

## Cover Letters

Katherine Hansen, associate publisher of QuintCareers.com, says writing autobiographical letters that specify the number of years you have spent in a field can backfire. "Significant or extensive experience" works just as well.

Use a cover letter to accentuate your adaptability to new situations, your enthusiasm, your "willingness to learn," as well as your reputation as a proven talent and team player. The AARP says cover letters should be as short as half a page and mention who referred you to the job (if this is the case), two or three accomplishments from your career that would make a good impression and your strong interest in the position. Be self-confident but not too boastful or too desperate, the organization suggests.

## Interviews

It's important to dress well and look sharp on the day of the interview.

As the questioning begins, always stress your skills and your experience. Stay away from starting any sentence with "when I was your age …" or "this is how we used to do that. …" Tell the interviewer you have significant problem-solving experience and would be happy to share your expertise with others. Hone in on a few examples revealing your prowess in getting things done.

Prior to entering the interview you should have updated your skills if necessary. As noted above, if the job requires computer skills, understanding the Microsoft Office suite, email and any other relevant programs is 

very important. If an application that you have not used comes up during the conversation, express solidly your willingness and eagerness to learn. Have one or two stories or examples in mind about how you were able to quickly master a new skill or task to solve an employer's problem. The adage "show don't tell" is worth revisiting during job interviews. People like stories, not just a dry recitation of facts from a long and fruitful career.

It is illegal for the interviewer to ask your age, unless you are interviewing for certain jobs such as an airline pilot. If you are asked about your age, the AARP suggests you respond by saying, "How do you see my age affecting my ability to do the job?" Do so in a polite, conservational, not-angry tone.

Finally, if you get the interview and you're speaking to a contemporary around your age, your comfort level will grow. But keep on guard in sharing too much about your career or your personal life. Stick to the topic at hand. A former newspaper boss recounts an excellent job candidate who lapsed into stories about her divorce. The interviewer felt a bit unnerved by the episode and worried that the same things could happen when she dealt with sources and with staff. After all, the interview only lasted an hour and he knew her entire life story.

Interviewees should not reveal details about their personal lives and should stay away from sharing gossip about people in their industries, even though they may think they're speaking to a confidante. When you've been in business for decades and you interview with a colleague, getting too chummy could backfire.

Remember, how you come across in an interview reveals your attitude — and to many employers, your attitude is just as important as your job skills when making an employment decision. Stay positive. Don't come across as a know-it-all, but do communicate that you can immediately add value.

Another issue in interviews is, of course, wages and benefits. Just because you have 30 years of experience doesn't mean you will receive more pay than a younger candidate.

## WAGES AND BENEFITS

AARP columnist Bob Skladany recommends you study any offers closely, without a sense of desperation. Look at your employment status (contract or regular employee), pay, health benefits, secondary benefits (disability and/or life insurance), paid time off, retirement savings plans, work schedule and potential for growth. Ask for this information in writing, even though it isn't required of employers.

## CASE STUDY:

### AN ENGINEER AND MARKETER

**Tom Bjorgum says many employers are** more than willing to overlook a few gray hairs if a job seeker has a world of good experience.

A Vietnam War veteran with a long career in engineering and marketing, Bjorgum, 59, lost his job at a motion automation company in 2008. He put together a chronological resume, worked the Internet job sites, networked through a job group at his church and hoped for the best.

When no offers came, Bjorgum received advice from a job search expert suggesting he write a skills-based resume, emphasizing his talent rather than career. He bought a resume software package and started over.

His new resume landed him an interview with a company that had posted a position on Monster.com. A week later, amazingly, he was sitting in an office entertaining a job offer from that company. (Bjorgum worked hard to improve his base salary, a strategy he describes in Chapter 10.)

The key to getting the job, he believes, was using a skills resume and only listing relatively recent jobs within the past 10 to 15 years, rather than his entire career. Having the rare combination of engineering and marketing helped.

"I felt I was in the driver's seat at the end, especially when I interviewed with the president of the company, and I felt there was a sense of urgency to get someone hired," he says. "I had good timing."

If you like the job, Skladany believes you should take it. If you have concerns, speak to the employer or recruiter while taking care not to ask too much. If the salary appears too low, first ask if the employer will entertain a counterproposal and then request a minimum of a 10 percent bump due to your expertise or experience. The employer has the right to say no, leaving you with the uncomfortable decision of whether to take it or leave it, he says. The key is to try for an improved contract that is "meaningful."

Negotiating for higher hourly wages is possible in the skilled trades, personal services, administrative and clerical areas, he says, but basic benefits are unlikely to be changed. You can ask for flexibility in scheduling and more training. For professional, salaried positions the opportunity for a higher salary, deferred compensation, incentive pay, stock options and other benefits is much higher. When vying for these jobs insist on a written employment agreement. Senior professional and upper management jobs offer the greatest negotiating opportunity on every aspect of employment.

## OTHER OPTIONS

It might be time to look at other options for your career path. This could mean embarking on a new career or self-employment. Starting your own business is a dream of many who never had an opportunity until becoming unemployed. You could start your dream business, buy an existing one or enlist in a franchise program.

Each of these career paths has an enviable advantage in that the only person who can fire you is yourself. The strategy comes, too, with a high failure rate.

An absolute requirement of the approach is that you will have to become an entrepreneur. You will have to find and nurture clients, manage business partners and staff, network, research, learn new skills and be a self-starter. Self-discipline is a necessity.

On the whole, the traits needed for exploring these options sound a lot like the activity involved in finding a job, don't they? Halfway through a job search you might decide to buy or start a business, grow one or become a consultant.

The leap toward consulting from job hunting isn't all that much of a stretch, especially since many job seekers consult while they look for jobs. Some even stop trying to find a job because they have become successful consultants and like the flexibility. They sometimes even surpass their previous salaries and can logoff early for a game of tennis, a bike ride or family needs.

Millions of Americans have found some satisfaction and success by going off on their own. It is still the American dream. It is not easy. It is not without real challenges, such as the cost of health insurance. Still, in a time when it can seem like no one will hire you, there is one person who can hire you — yourself. It may be a time to go for it.

# NOTES

# The Job Interview

*"Success is where preparation and opportunity meet."*

— BOBBY UNSER, FORMER INDY 500 CHAMPION

So you've come to that cherished moment in your job search when your hard work has paid off and you received the call to come in for an interview. Now is the time for yet more preparation. You will have to brush up on the employer by doing research, start a list of anticipated questions, and practice answering questions and interviewing.

You will have to make your personal appearance a priority and get into a mentally alert frame of mind before walking into an interview room to face someone who might be your manager someday.

You have to look smart, think smart and be ready. "Success is the result of perfection, hard work, learning from failure, loyalty and persistence," said Colin Powell, former U.S. secretary of state and retired four-star general. And Benjamin Franklin probably offered the best summation for anyone pursuing a goal in life: "By failing to prepare, you are preparing to fail."

## INTERVIEW PREPARATION

Knowing the kind of information the employer is likely to seek will help you prepare for the interview. Employers want to know your motivation for employment, your ability to do the job, how you will fit into the organization and how much you will cost them. Being able to answer probing questions in these areas will make for a successful interview. And being able to ask good questions and look for opportunities to show off your knowledge of the company you're interviewing with can make all the difference in the world.

A great advantage is to have as much information as you can about the position and the company before that first interview. It will help you to target your skills to the specific needs of the employer and demonstrate your enthusiasm for the job. Companies, after all, have limited information from which to make a decision — an application or resume, references and several interviews. It's up to YOU to convince the employer you are the best person for the job. Be prepared to connect your skills, experience, training and education to what the hiring manager needs in a new hire.

Prior to walking in the door, you should cover a few of the following areas on your own.

## Do Your Research

When on the phone arranging your interview, do a little interviewing yourself. Ask about the interview process, who you will be interviewing with (one person or a panel) and how long it will take. Ask if you can see the full job description again and inquire if the company needs any supporting documentation. Get the address of the interview location (companies have multiple sites, and going to the wrong one is a major slip up) and the office and mobile phone number of the interviewer just in case you blow a tire on the freeway on the way there.

On your own, study the company's website, brochures, annual business reports, trade periodicals, manufacturer's guides and any other materials you can find. Good sources for finding that information were covered in Chapter 2, but generally the three spots are libraries, Minnesota WorkForce Centers and the Internet.

## Match Your Skills to the Job

Once you've gathered what you need to know about the employer, look at the job description again and study how your skills, experience and employment history match what the company requests. By coupling your strengths with their list of desired traits, you might be halfway

there — well, you must be, or they would not have asked you for the interview.

If you're deficient in an area, you must be ready to convince the employer you can and will learn the skill. You could also show how your other skills will make up for this weakness or have non-work examples of the trait, such as being a volunteer leader of a nonprofit group or committee. Another strategy is to have a plan of action to overcome the deficiency. Don't have Web design skills? Knowing when and where you can enroll in a Web design course in your community may convince the employer you're the right person to hire.

## Find Your Attitude

Employers are looking for people with a positive work attitude. Often employers emphasize attitude over skills, training and experience. Look for ways to show your enthusiasm for the job, willingness to learn, spirit of cooperation and respect for the employer. Review your skills for reinforcement of your qualifications. Rehearse how you'll present yourself. Be positive, truthful and realistic.

Athletes call it their "game face." And make sure to have it for the interview, says Letetia Klebel, human resources manager of Pro Fabrication in Madison, Minn. Klebel says she sees many people who haven't interviewed in 15 years. She suggests coming in with a good attitude, and try to be relaxed. And be willing and able to ask questions. "I can't believe how many people come in for professional jobs and don't have any questions for us," says Klebel. "You should always come prepared with a couple of questions to ask us about the company and our jobs."

## Look Good

An important part of the impression you make on an employer is your physical appearance. An employer might reason that the person who doesn't care about her/his appearance won't care about the job. Neat, clean and conservative is a safe standard for dress and grooming. No matter what kind of job you are applying for you should look as professional as possible, including footwear. You may not be applying for a job that requires a suit, but for the interview you may want to try to be, for a day, the best-dressed person to visit the employer's office or plant. Here's an introduction on looking good:

- Get a good night's sleep
- Take a shower the morning of the interview
- Shave
- Brush your teeth
- Comb your hair
- Clean your fingernails
- Wear clean and pressed clothes
- Wear proper clothes and shoes for the job
- Clean and shine your shoes
- Do not wear flip-flops or sneakers
- Conceal or take out body piercings
- Avoid smoking before the interview
- Do not chew gum during an interview
- Do not wear sunglasses
- Do not wear fragrances

### INTERVIEW CLOTHING TIPS FOR WOMEN

Either pants, suits or skirted suits are appropriate. Skirt length should be at or just below the knee. Make sure your clothing is not too tight and avoid cleavage and perfume. Keep make-up and nail polish simple and conservative, jewelry conservative and minimal. Wear clean, low-heeled shoes and stay away from faddish clothing.

### INTERVIEW CLOTHING TIPS FOR MEN

Make sure your belt matches your shoes, keep facial hair neatly trimmed and match a decent tie to your suit or sports coat. Comb your hair neatly, wear dress shoes and don't smell like a cologne ad.

## TYPES OF INTERVIEWS

The purpose of an interview is to get acquainted and to learn about one another. Employers evaluate your qualifications, and you get to provide a human face to a resume and a phone call, as well as sell the employer on your skills, experience and enthusiasm. But the interview is not just about you; it's also about them. It is an opportunity for you to learn more about the job — what it is really like — and find out if you really want it. Moreover, you will discover whether this is a company you will enjoy working for.

Three common types of interviews are telephone screening, in-person screening and the selection interview. It doesn't matter what type of interview you face; what matters is that you present your qualifications to the final decision maker while maintaining good relations with everyone you come into contact with, from the staff at the waiting area to receptionists and parking lot attendants. If you're lucky, you may see them all again when you get the job.

### Telephone Screening Interview

This interview saves the employer time by eliminating candidates based on essential criteria such as employment objective, education or required skills. Since these interviews will often occur unexpectedly, it's important your job search records are organized and kept where you can reach them at a moment's notice. If you are unprepared, simply ask if you can call back in five minutes, or have them call back. It's not an unreasonable demand, and the employer may be impressed that you seek to be prepared instead of just winging the interview.

### In-person Screening Interview

The company can verify your qualifications for the position and establish a preliminary impression of attitude, interest and professional style. A professional screener from the employer's human resources department most often conducts the interview. At this stage, the goal is to select candidates to meet with the decision maker. You still have to perform well during the interview and leave a good impression.

### Selection Interview

Conducted by the decision maker, this interview will probe your qualifications and assess your comfort level with the challenges of the position and other team members. There may be more than one interview at this stage. As the candidates are whittled down, you may be invited back to speak with the same person and with other managers or members of a work group. Your ability to establish rapport and present yourself as the right person is critical.

Even with just one interviewer, opinions of the others will be sought and may have an effect on the outcome. When you're invited to interview with a number of people, it's important to present yourself effectively to each one of them. Remember, they will be evaluating your skills and ability to fit in. As always, be yourself, but sell to each person's concerns.

## Behavioral Interview

Traditional interview questions, such as "tell me about yourself," offer employers limited information about your qualifications. Behavioral interviewing can provide more information about your on-the-job behavior, personality and character. The interviewer will ask questions that require you to describe how you have handled work-related situations. For instance, a question might be: "Describe a time when you had to overcome a stressful work situation and how you dealt with it." From an employer's perspective, behavioral interviewing gives more insight about your potential than traditional questions.

Sometimes this technique is called STAR, which stands for "Situation, Task, Action and Results." That's the order you will follow should you encounter an interviewer who uses the STAR method. It's a good idea to think of a few STAR stories ahead of time that you can adapt to different behavioral interviewing questions. Remember the importance of being authentic and real. Don't say anything like, "Well, I never had the kind of problems in my past job that you want me to address here." The interviewer will know that is unlikely.

Take it as a chance to tell a story that illustrates your skills and offers the interviewer insights that give a good impression of you. As you tell your STAR stories, employers will listen for evidence of the skills required for the job. By now you've done plenty of research about the position, and the STAR method allows you to show employers you possess the skills they need.

## Work Sample Interview

This type of interview gives applicants an opportunity to show what they have done at previous jobs. It could be the place for graphic artists to display portfolios and salespeople to make a sales presentation. (Even better, do as one job expert suggests, and bring potential sales leads to the interview!) An office worker may be asked to complete a business letter using a specific type of computer software program. An editor might be asked to edit a document.

## Peer Group Interview

This is an opportunity to meet and talk with your prospective coworkers. Just as in other interviews, the peer group will be evaluating you, determining how you fit in.

## Group Interview

This type of interview takes place with a group of other candidates, and usually more than one interviewer. Introduce yourself to other candidates and, of course, be polite. Try to show confidence by volunteering to respond first to a few questions, but do not dominate the entire interview. To show your ability to be a team player, compliment another candidate's response and then build on it with your own thoughts. Direct your answer to the individual asking the question, but try to maintain some eye contact with the other members of the group. Don't forget to smile.

## Luncheon or Coffee Interview

This type of interview assesses how well you can handle yourself in a social situation. Employer representatives may include the hiring manager, a human resource department member and one or more peer employees. Choose your meal selection carefully. Spilling on your blouse or tie isn't likely to make a favorable impression. Select healthy and easy things to eat so you can answer questions and pay attention to the conversation.

If the interview is conducted at a coffee shop — and a fair number of interviews are these days — the setting probably has more to do with the hiring manager than anything else. He or she wants to escape the office and speak to you in a casual, informal atmosphere that will likely make for an honest discussion of your strengths and weaknesses. Try not to consider if others are listening in — they probably are — and use the time to reveal your commitment to the industry and your desire to work for the company.

## Stress Interview

A stress interview re-creates some challenging situations you might run into on the job. The interviewer asks you a number of tough questions that are designed to make you somewhat uncomfortable. For example, he or she might present a job-related scenario and ask you to explain how you would respond. Keep your cool, take your time in responding to the questions and reward yourself when it's all over. Don't take it personally. This is usually a test of whether you can handle stress on the job and can assess a complicated question quickly.

## Video Conference Interview

Some employers today use video conferences to conduct meetings or carry out other aspects of their business, such as interviewing candidates who live in other states or communities a good distance from where they are located. Conducting an interview via video conference enables an employer to save travel costs and still have, in effect, a person-to-person interview. If the thought of facing a camera during an interview frightens you, practice video conferencing beforehand or in front of a mirror.

## COMMUNICATE YOUR BEST IMAGE

Get everything organized early. Fill out applications neatly, completely and in black ink. If requested, collect letters of recommendation, your reference list, copies of licenses, driving record (for those jobs that require it) and Social Security or Alien Registration card. Bring a notebook, pen, business cards and extra copies of your resume. Bring your portfolio, and if you have a Web-based version, write down the URL so you can find it rapidly.

And put it all in a nice folder, zippered case or briefcase. Look professional.

Arrive on time for the interview. Plan your schedule and route so you arrive 10 to 15 minutes prior to the appointment time. Do not — repeat, do not — arrive a half hour early or an hour early to show your desire for the job. Your interviewers are likely to find this irritating because they may have to change their schedule to handle your earlier arrival. They gave you an interview time for a reason, and show up a few minutes before it, and no more.

While you are sitting in the lobby, review questions you want to ask in the interview, your resume and your personal data record for related skills. By now you should have convinced yourself you are the best person for the job. Now it's time to convince the employer.

## Send Good Signals

The vast majority of communication is nonverbal. Your posture, walk, dress, facial movement, energy, gestures and eye contact are all nonverbal signals. Try using a natural greeting and shake hands firmly, but only if a hand is offered to you first. Show reserved confidence and let the interviewer start the dialogue.

Focus on the questions and answer carefully. When your chance comes ask good questions about the job, the company and the team you may be joining.

Every interview is a learning experience. Use each one as a building block for the next one. You may go through many interviews before you connect with the right job. You should get better with practice. Analyze what went right and what went wrong with every interview, and then ensure that the surprise question or the strange inquiry during the next one does not throw you off course.

## Show and Tell

You may be a good worker, but you have to back up statements with samples demonstrating your productivity and accomplishments in past jobs. Tell employers about your skills, because no one else will. Let employers know you can adjust, work well with others, and fit into a new environment without complaints. Tell a story from your experience that illustrates your flexibility.

Stories are important. "When you interview, tell stories. You know you're going to encounter the question, 'What are your strengths?' Don't give a list," writes Penelope Truck in "Brazen Careerists." "It's not persuasive. Tell a story about your strengths. This way you tell the hiring manager something memorable and you get in a bit about your achievements."

You should emphasize your commitment to learning. Demonstrate this through your own independent study, professional development, education, workshops and awards. Your plan for future development also communicates your commitment to learning.

## Finish Strong

Demonstrate interest by asking when the position will be filled. In the final stage, summarize why you're qualified by stating strengths and qualities you may have forgotten to emphasize earlier. Remember, don't overstay your time.

Ask what the next step is in the hiring process. Will there be additional interviews? When will the hiring decision be made? When could you call back for the decision? Be proactive in your follow-up. Schedule the next interview. Arrange to call the employer to learn the decision.

## Follow-up

Evaluate the interview. What went well in the interview? How can you improve?

Record your follow-up plans. Write the date and time for your next contact with the employer. Be sure you follow through on these plans.

Send thank you letters, notes or emails within 24 hours to each person with whom you interviewed. For information on thank you letters and notes, see the next chapter entitled Finishing Touches.

# KEY INTERVIEW QUESTIONS

Employers use all kinds of interview strategies. We will look at typical questions and then delve into those that require more attention to storytelling and detail, and the ones that tease out valuable clues about how you would fit into a work environment.

### Can you tell me about yourself?

This is an open-ended question often asked to help break the ice in the interview. The important thing to remember is to keep the answer job-related. Your response to this question should last about two minutes and be especially well-practiced.

### Why are you interested in working for this company?

This will show the employer you've done your homework. State the positive things you've learned about the company and how they fit with your career goals. Mention you just read an article or saw a piece on the news about the company. Highlight that you were impressed by the performance of a particular unit, or the entire company, over the past year. "Your sales increase of 20 percent was impressive," goes a long way toward showing you did your research.

### Can you tell me about your education?

Even though your resume includes this information, some employers want you expand on the subject. Mention your grade point if it was over 3.0 and what impact your education has had on your understanding of the world and of your professional field. Always note the classes, seminars, workshops and on-the-job training you've attended that support your job goals.

### Why have you chosen this particular field?

This is one way to show your enthusiasm and dedication to your career. Share your continued excitement to be a nurse, or a technologist, or a teacher or a truck driver.

### Can you describe your best and worst bosses?

This could be a trap. Don't present a negative picture of any past employers. If given a choice, always talk about your best boss. If pressed to describe the worst boss, pick a work-related characteristic that can be stated in a positive way. For example, "I had a supervisor who was vague when issuing assignments. I learned to ask questions so that I knew what was expected."

### In a job, what interests you the most and the least?

This will give the employer another gauge for measuring how well you will fit the job opening.

### What is your major weakness?

"I have none" won't work or will come off as less than honest. Turn the question into a positive by stating how you overcame a weakness. Martin Yate, author of "Knock 'em Dead, the Ultimate Search Guide," gives an illustration where a job seeker admits to not always handling paperwork well. His manager tells him to work on getting the paperwork in order. He "takes it to heart" and changes his behavior and notes, "You only have to

tell me something once." The scenario, adds Yate, offers you the added bonus of "showing that you accept and act on criticism."

### Can you give an example of how you solved a problem in the past?

It's important to be able to show the process you go through when presented with a problem. State the problem and the steps you followed to reach the solution. If it's hard to come up with a problem, switch to a project and how you completed it.

### What are your strengths?

This is the time to describe the skills you've identified that will most effectively market you as an employee. Offer a confident and measured response, delineating skills or skill sets and how they have led to your success in past jobs and will benefit another employer in the future.

### How do others describe you?

Another way for the employer to ask this would be, "How would you fit into this work group?" If you aren't comfortable with this question or don't know how to answer it, call some friends or people you've worked with and ask them to describe you.

### What do you consider the most important idea you contributed or your most noteworthy accomplishment in your last job?

Give examples of ways in which you saved the employer time or money, or developed an office procedure that improved efficiency. Any leadership opportunities should be illuminated.

## Where do you see yourself in three years?

Telling the interviewer "In your job!" isn't a good idea. Do indicate that you hope to acquire sufficient skills and knowledge within that time to make a positive contribution to the company. You might pick a position a step or two above the post you are applying for, but tell the interviewer you only want a promotion you have earned and one in which you will have the confidence to succeed.

## How do you think you will fit into this operation?

This is the time to express your interest in the job and knowledge of the employer. The more you know about the operation the easier this question will be to answer.

## If you were hired, what ideas/ talents could you contribute to the position or our company?

This is another great opportunity for you to sell your skills. By giving examples of past accomplishments, you help the employer visualize your contribution to the company.

## Can you give an example where you showed leadership and initiative?

Even if you haven't had the title of lead worker, supervisor or manager, give examples of when you recognized a job needed to be done and you did it. Again, use samples outside the workforce if they fit.

## Give me an example of when you were able to contribute to a team project?

Any job that requires communicating with others usually requires some amount of teamwork. For example, teamwork is used in sales because both parties have to state their needs and expectations before negotiating the sale. Families, community activities and school all require teamwork.

## What have you done to develop or change in the last few years?

This shows a willingness to be challenged and to improve. Employers are looking for people who are willing to continue learning. Talk about formal and informal educational opportunities you've pursued. Mention books and periodicals you've read related to your field of interest.

## Do you have any questions for me?

By asking questions, you again show interest in the job. Listed later in this chapter are some questions you may want to ask at your interview.

- Keep your answers brief and job-related.
- Focus on your skills.
- Help the employer see you in the job.

## THE TOUGHEST QUESTIONS

Give direct, honest answers. Take your time. Develop the answer in your head before you respond. If you don't understand a question, ask for it to be repeated or clarified. You don't have to rush, but don't be indecisive.

Ask questions in return.

Be prepared. Answering difficult questions that may reflect negatively on you can be answered by using the "sandwich model." This model has a positive statement followed by admitting the negative situation, and ending with another positive statement about what you've done to overcome the problem. Ending with a positive statement leaves a positive impression. Anticipate tough questions and practice interviewing beforehand.

### Why were you let go?

Try a few of these examples as a tactic to answering this hardest of questions.

My skills are in engineering (or name your field). My employer decided those skills were no longer needed. Therefore, I've taken some training and upgraded my skills (specify) to meet the qualifications for this type of job.

Or, if you were fired, career expert and columnist Joyce Lain Kennedy suggests several great answers, among them the following.

- I was cut loose and that was a blessing because I got a chance to explore different opportunities like the one we're talking about right now.

- My competencies weren't a good match with my former employer's needs.

- The job simply wasn't working out for my boss and me, and we both agreed it was time to move on.

- The former job was a learning experience, and I'm wiser now and want a chance to prove it.

- A new manager came in and cleaned house, including me, and I figured it was time to move on, anyway.

- Certain personal problems that I have surmounted upset my work life. I'm now up and running strong to exceed expectations in a new job. I wanted to move my career in a different direction and that set up the conditions for departure.

- I usually hit it off with bosses, but this time was an exception. We didn't hit it off and I'm not sure why.

- My job was offshored to India. I outlasted several downsizings but not the last one.

- I was desperate for work and took the wrong job.

"Keep it brief, keep it honest and keep it moving," she suggests.

### *It appears you haven't worked in the last five years or 10 years. Why?*

I've been busy going to school full time (specify), raising two children and managing my home. Doing that on a daily basis gave me a lot of skills we generally don't acknowledge, like leadership, time management, teaching, coordination, planning and so forth.

I needed to address some health issues. It would not have been fair to an employer if I took too much time off from work. I'm now ready to return to work and give you 100 percent.

I was trained in machine operation while at a correctional facility. I have now completed my GED® and am ready to work for you.

## ASKING QUESTIONS IN INTERVIEWS

When Karen Oldenborg went for an interview with the St. Francis School District, she had a couple of ideas of how to deal with tough questions.

She'd ask them herself.

In an interview for an administrative post in the district, Oldenborg asked a panel of school officials what weakness they saw in her resume. "You don't have a lot of experience in tracking things," one school official noted.

Oldenborg, 47, responded this way: "That's a good point. But I have learned multiple computer systems over the years and I am not afraid to jump in. When I have an issue with a system I only will ask you once."

At the end of the interview, the panel asked Oldenborg if she had any questions. "Yes, I have six," she said, before proceeding to ask about her duties, an average day on the job and other "process-related" inquiries.

"They looked at me with that 'oh, this is going to take a while,'" Oldenborg recalls with a laugh. She also asked panel members to spell their names so she could send each of them a thank you card.

As it turns out, the gesture wasn't necessary. Four hours after the interview, a school district official called and offered her the job, and nine months of unemployment finally ended.

---

**Questions to Ask in an Interview**

- Would you describe an average day on this job?

- What is the history of the position? Why is it vacant?

- What aspects of this job would you like to see performed better?

- What are the key challenges or problems of this position?

- Can the duties of this position be expanded?

- Where can I go from here, assuming I meet/exceed the job responsibilities?

- How would you describe the ideal candidate?

- What are the employer's short- and long-range objectives?

- What are some outside influences that affect company growth?

- Where does the company excel? What are its limitations?

- When and how will I be evaluated? What are the performance standards?

- With whom would I be working? Who would be my supervisor? Who would I supervise?

- What is the department's environment like?

- When will you make the hiring decision? May I call you for the decision? When is a good time?

## ILLEGAL AND LEGAL QUESTIONS

Questions asked in an interview should focus on your qualifications for the job. Federal and state laws help ensure you aren't asked illegal questions, but occasionally they do come up on an application or in an interview. Some employers may not have a clear understanding of federal and state rules and inquire into areas that are legally off limits.

Questions should be job-related and not used to find out personal information. Employers should not ask about any of the following, because to not hire a candidate because of any one of them is discriminatory:

- Race
- Color
- Sex
- Religion
- National origin
- Birthplace
- Age
- Disability
- Marital/family status
- Genetic information

## Illegal Questions

For the candidate, it's a good idea to have a plan of action ready if illegal job interview questions are ever asked. Think through possible illegal questions ahead of time and decide how you will handle them.

If you encounter illegal questions, you can be prepared to respond. You are attempting to determine why the interviewer is asking such a question. If you know the intent of the question, then you can reply with an appropriate answer. For example, if you are asked whether you are a United States citizen (not legal to ask), reply that you are authorized to work in the U.S., which is a question the employer can ask you and which is appropriate to answer.

**Federal laws such as the Civil Rights Act and the Americans With Disabilities Act, as well as state law, prohibit the following questions:**

- Do you prefer to go by Miss, Mrs. or Ms.?
- What is your maiden name?
- What is your native language and the language you speak at home?
- What is your ancestry?
- How many children do you have?
- Do you plan to have more children?
- How do you plan to care for your children while on the job?
- What is or was your spouse's name or line of work?
- Have you ever filed a workers' compensation claim or been injured on the job?
- Do you have any physical impairments that would prevent you from performing the job for which you're applying?
- Have you ever been arrested?
- What is your religion?
- What is your hair/eye color? What is your height/weight?
- Have you ever been hospitalized? If so, for what condition?
- Have you ever been treated by a psychiatrist or psychologist? If so, for what condition?
- Is there any health-related reason you may not be able to perform the job for which you're applying?
- How many days were you absent from work because of illness last year?
- Are you taking any prescribed drugs?
- Have you ever been treated for drug addiction or alcoholism?

## Resources

Most illegal questioning is not deliberate. However, any individual who believes that his or her employment rights have been violated may file a charge of discrimination with the EEOC or the Minnesota Department of Human Rights by contacting:

Equal Employment Opportunity Commission
www.eeoc.gov
(612) 335-4040 (Minneapolis Area Office)
800-669-4000

Minnesota Department of Human Rights
http://mn.gov/mdhr
(651) 539-1100
800-657-3704

## Perfectly Legal Questions

You can expect to hear one or more of the following questions, which are perfectly legal. In other parts of this book and this chapter, we address difficult questions that pose challenges, especially if you are an ex-offender looking for a chance to right your life.

- What is your current address and phone contact?
- Describe your education.
- What experience qualifies you for this job?
- Do you have licenses/certifications for this job?
- Are you willing to travel?
- What name(s) are your work records under?
- Are you available for overtime?
- Do you have the legal right to work in the United States?
- Have you served in the U.S. armed forces?
- Do you have any convictions other than misdemeanors?

## REASONS YOU DIDN'T GET HIRED

Usually people don't get hired due to a simple reality: For that job the employer found someone more qualified or who met certain specifications you didn't possess. Sometimes it is as simple as that. Don't beat up yourself too badly if everything seemed to have gone right. It may have. It just went better for someone else.

While the preceding reason is most common, here are a few other reasons people do not get hired: inability to express skills and information clearly, lack of interest and enthusiasm, lack of confidence and poise, over-aggressiveness, too much emphasis on money, poor personal appearance, unwillingness to start at the bottom, or lack of tact and courtesy.

It is reasonable to seek feedback from the employer about why you did not land the job, particularly if you went far in the interview process. That information can help you hone your job interview skills for next time.

# CHAPTER 10

# Finishing Touches

*"Silent gratitude isn't much use to anyone."*

— G.B. STERN, NOVELIST

Every job search needs finishing touches — those often overlooked actions likely to impress potential employers even if you don't get the job this time around. They show an attention to detail, an admirable and non-irritating persistence, and a genuine civility beyond just trying to use contacts and interviewers to find employment.

Applied regularly and teamed with appropriate skills and qualifications, a graceful finishing touch should eventually lead employers to see you as a potential hire, worthy of a second look and perhaps a job offer.

Just as accountants take the time to scrutinize their work one last time, job seekers should write thank you letters and other correspondences to continue their sales campaigns to land jobs.

A thoughtful note gives you one last chance to leave an outstanding and memorable impression on the employer. If done correctly, these steps can put you a cut above the competition. It shows initiative and care to complete the sales process, so to speak, even though potential employers may not see it precisely in that way. You should see it that way because finding a job, in the end, is all about selling you.

## POST-INTERVIEW STEPS

After spending all that time preparing for an interview and successfully sailing through it, do not drop the ball in the final hours. Here's a simple two-part approach that will take little time and yield great benefits by leaving an unmistakably good impression.

### Contacting References

If your interview went well, you should contact your references to prepare them for a potential phone call or email from the employer. You might recap the interview briefly to each reference and highlight any points you made that they can verify, or emphasize, should they be asked by the interviewer for a testimony to your skills, experience and character.

You might end up saying something like this to a reference: "Jim, the company seemed really interested in the management skills I provided for the business development projects we worked on from 2010 to 2013. If asked, could you elaborate and stress the important role I had during that time? You may recall it was a small team. No one volunteered to manage the projects except me, and they all turned out pretty successful."

It should be a given that references will agree with your point of view. If you have to persuade them, make sure they agree, in the end, with your perceptions. References can say the same good things about you, but you should remind them with an example or two of the kinds of qualities you possess.

During the interview, if you mentioned strong communication skills, then have one of your references highlight that trait and point to a project in which your writing and speaking skills were exercised to a good end. If you showed up at work on time, always did what was told, always pitched in when needed, then a reference should be able to back you up on those traits.

## Thank You Notes, Emails and Letters

Saying "thank you" in your job search isn't only an effective job search strategy, it's the right thing to do. Every thank you note or letter is an opportunity to sell your qualifications again. Sending a card or letter after an interview is common, but don't spare your thank you notes during the job hunt. Express your gratitude to employment contacts, members of your network and references who have extended themselves on your behalf, from informational interviewers to those who offer referrals or information.

Thank you may be said in person, by phone, an informal note such as a simple handwritten card, in a letter written on a word processor or by email. Overall, handwritten notes work best because they are the most personal form of communication unless your handwriting tends to be sloppy. The thank you letter should follow a standard business letter format. To add style to it try using a less formal font. The situation and your personal style will determine which one you send.

At the minimum, a thank you note or letter should be sent after all interviews. This is your chance to make one more impression before the decision is made. Send a thank you note even if you're turned down for a job. Let employers know you appreciate their consideration, and you'd be interested in future opportunities.

Some people may wonder if an email is too impersonal for a thank you. Write both types of notes if you're really interested in getting the job. Craft a brief email after the interview and then drop a thank you card to the company within 24 hours. Try not to be too overly enthusiastic in your thanks. Be professional, express your continued interest in the job and in working for the company, and mention your appreciation for the interview.

## IF YOU GET TURNED DOWN

Upon receiving a phone call or letter of rejection, let interviewers know that although you're disappointed you're still interested in working for the employer. That is, if you are. If you are only marginally attracted to the company, be honest with yourself and do not follow up with the interviewer with any "still love to work with you" communications. But thank him or her for the consideration, of course.

Should you still have desires to work for the employer, thank the interviewer for the time and interest, re-emphasize your interest in openings and ask if you could continue to maintain contact. Find out if there are, or might be, other openings or other people you could contact.

Many times the person selected ends up turning down the job or doesn't work out. Keep the communication line open, positive and professional. This keeps your name in their mind for the next opening.

_Stay positive_. Congratulate yourself. You did get the interview, which means the employer was interested in you. Learn from the experience. Ask for feedback from the interviewer on what you could improve or do differently.

_Keep trying_. This isn't the time to stop. Forge ahead. Don't despair. Getting turned down happens to all of us at some point in our lives. It's up to you to decide which tips will work best for you.

## THE SALARY NEGOTIATION

Let's say your first interview with a prospective employer leads to further discussions. Congratulations. You are moving ahead in the process. Next you may face additional interviews and, inevitably, a conversation about compensation.

If an employer asks how much you expect to be compensated, give a salary range instead of a definite number. Come to the interview prepared with knowledge of a reasonable salary range for the position. Use a career information website to learn about the salary range for related positions. Otherwise, contacting the human resources office or a networking contact that works in the company may be helpful.

Let the employer bring up salary first and try to avoid the issue entirely in the initial interview. Delaying salary negotiation as long as possible allows you to better understand what the position entails before the question of salary is addressed. It also gives you more time to articulate what you'll bring to the employer before an offer is made.

The next step is salary negotiation. It can set the tone for your work life and experience with the employer. These are some suggestions to consider when you receive a job offer. Negotiating is a two-way street. Try to achieve a win-win situation. It's up to you to decide which tips will work best for you.

## WHEN YOU GET THE JOB

Should you get the job, congratulate yourself and then look closely at the offer you are receiving. If the job is a good fit and the salary and benefits meet your expectations, you may be inclined to accept it. On the other hand, if you think the salary is too low or the benefits are not quite right, you can negotiate for a better contract.

You may not get it, and you could run the risk of losing the opportunity. But many employers anticipate that some applicants will advocate for a stronger compensation package.

## Negotiating Tips

Founder of Quintessential Careers and www. quintcareers.com, Randall S. Hansen, a job negotiation expert, urges you to know the salary you can reasonably accept and expect, based on your experience and education and on industry wage standards. Some online sources, such as www.salary.com, can help you determine the

## PROFILE:

### TIPS FOR NEGOTIATING A HIGHER SALARY

**When Tom Bjorgum finally found** a job in the nation's worst recession in decades, he liked everything about it except one thing: the salary.

The company that eventually hired him, a power transmission distributor, offered a salary half the amount he once earned. Bjorgum, 59, figured he could negotiate a higher annual salary and a better deal on the bonus payout that occurred twice a year.

A few advantages played into his favor, among them a distinguished career in engineering sales and a potential employer who wanted someone to start quickly in the newly created job. It did not hurt, either, that two competitors for the position were dropped for different reasons.

And Bjorgum had a good argument.

"I did some research on salaries of sales engineers in the Twin Cities. It showed the average was $83,000 a year," he says. "That helped in negotiations. I figured I was in the driver's seat because I had interviewed with the president of the company, and I felt there was a sense of urgency to get someone in to start selling. It was good timing for me."

With the salary data in hand and his new employer needing to ignite some sales, Bjorgum asked for $10,000 to be added to his salary and for a larger percent in bonuses. The employer agreed to the terms. "I did the research online and I gave it to them," he says. "I thought the job was mine to lose, but I wasn't trying to be greedy."

salaries in certain jobs and fields based on years of experience. Never attend a job negotiation without knowing the average salary range in your field and at the company where you're applying. Where you live matters, too. The larger the city and the higher the cost of living, the more likely you'll receive a bigger salary.

Express your appreciation and strong interest in the job. Request at least 24 hours to consider it, even when saying "yes." Ask any questions you need clarified. Assess the job offer in terms of your needs, benefits and long-term career and life goals. Talk it over with someone you respect. Make a list of the pros and cons of the job offer.

"The job search these days drags on longer and longer. When you finally obtain that offer after weeks and weeks (and in some cases, months), it's not unusual to want to accept it right on the spot," writes Hansen on his website. "But even the best offers should be reviewed when you have a clear head — and without the pressure of your future boss or HR director staring at you. Most employers are willing to give you some time to contemplate a job offer — typically several days to a week."

Make sure the job description is clear. Note your reporting relationships, authority and advancement potential. Keep asking questions until you clearly understand. Careful thought and consideration will only gain you respect.

If you want the job, make it clear to the employer. If you're uncertain, state there are some items you'd like to discuss before you can accept the job and suggest meeting further to talk about the offer.

Focus your negotiations on a couple of items that are priorities for you. Items that could be negotiable include salary, benefits, tuition, training and vacation time, as well as a flexible schedule, stock options, company car, onsite day care and parking privileges. A compensation package is not just a salary. It includes health care and many other benefits that may be of greater value to you than a higher salary.

Today, many job seekers want good health insurance more than any other benefit. Ask what policies are available to you with the employer and then, on your own, consider how much that insurance would cost you with another employer with a weaker policy.

If you want more vacation time or a more flexible schedule, you may have to give up a little compensation — and you will have to decide if that's a deal you can live with.

Negotiations should never become emotional or hostile. Use your value, skills, experience and education to negotiate. Listen carefully. If the offer is less than you expected, let them know and state you're still interested in the position if they want to reconsider their offer. Don't assume the first offer is fixed even if the interviewer tells you it is.

If the same figure is offered a couple days later you can ask for a salary review in six months to evaluate your performance to determine if a salary bump is in order. Or, you can turn down the job while maintaining cheerful relations by asking that they keep you in mind for future openings paying a larger salary.

When you reach an agreement, request a document in writing and study it to make sure it contains the agreed upon points. And then have a celebration.

# HOW TO SUCCEED ON THE JOB

 Once you've made the big transition from job searching to landing the job, your next goal is job success. There are specific skills you need to know and use to be successful at your new position. Start by checking with your supervisor to determine your most important tasks and on what attributes you will be judged in reviews. Employers say more people lose their job due to poor work habits, rather than inability to do the work. The following suggestions are based on feedback culled from employers.

## Employer Expectations

A positive attitude is one of the most important factors in achieving job success. Don't carry negative feelings into your new workplace. Deal with those emotions elsewhere.

*Always be on time*. How long will it take to get to work? Allow a few extra minutes for traffic problems and getting children to child care. Set an alarm clock to help you get up. Reliability and dependability will help you gain trust and respect from your new employer.

*Strive for good attendance*. If you need to be out sick, ask your supervisor the proper method of notification.

*Know and follow* all workplace rules, policies and procedures. Read the employee manuals.

*Listen and learn*. Be open to new ways of doing things, even if you were taught differently in school or on a different job. Don't be quick to find fault, criticize or complain until you can prove you can do something a better way.

*Meet and exceed* your employer's expectations. And if the expectations aren't clear, ask your employer to define them.

*Learn all you can* about your job before thinking about moving up the career ladder. Keep in mind you might not enjoy every aspect of your new job. Overcoming challenges at work may be still more appealing than not having a job at all. Now, let's look at several crucial areas in job performance.

## Communication

A key component of any job is communication. When you need to talk with your supervisor, ask when would be a good time to meet. Consider your performance reviews opportunities for personal growth. Ask how you can improve. Most supervisors appreciate employees who are concerned about performance and want to improve. Your job success is also their success.

Ask for help when you need it. If you make a mistake, let your supervisor know immediately. Find out how you can fix it. Follow the proper chain of command. Discuss issues with your supervisor first.

## Personal

Prior to starting the job, complete all of your appointments with doctors, dentists and others. Have an emergency plan for child care and transportation.

Be willing to learn new skills. Keep a record of classes you're taking that relate to the job. Review this with your supervisor when appropriate.

Take time in making new friends. Find positive and upbeat coworkers. Avoid negative, critical and gossiping people.

Be clean and well-groomed. Wear clean and job-appropriate clothes. Pay attention to how your coworkers are dressed. Avoid wearing strong fragrances.

Keep your personal life and problems at home. Don't use the employer's equipment and time for checking personal email, making personal phone calls, using the copy machine or resolving your personal problems on the job. If you're having trouble resolving personal problems, counseling,

support groups or employee assistance programs may be useful.

Be patient with yourself and your employer. It takes time to become familiar with a new job and learn the ins and outs. It often takes a good six months before you understand and feel comfortable with every task, your team members, clients and responsibilities.

If an opportunity presents itself you should volunteer for projects and committees if your supervisor approves. These experiences will give you a chance to exercise talents that aren't required in your current position and help you create a larger network of contacts within a company if your volunteer role is internal. In case of an external volunteer assignment, you will see the same advantages while building a professional network of contacts that could help you find a job in the future.

## Getting Along With Others

Always respect diversity in the workplace, recognizing that people with different backgrounds often come together to produce better outcomes.

Accept criticism as constructive. Don't become defensive or take criticism personally. Thank people for their input. Consider changing your behavior if it's warranted. If you're unsure how to handle a situation, check with your supervisor. Always be friendly to everyone and be willing to go the extra mile. This creates goodwill with employers, coworkers and customers.

Notice who your boss respects and model yourself after them. Find a mentor, someone who knows the employer and the job well enough to coach you or show you the ropes.

Show appreciation. Let your supervisor(s) know you appreciate their training, support, input and feedback. Some bosses want to hear, too, real results that may not be favorable to them, or you. That requires a level of honesty that can be difficult to display but is intrinsic to your success and that of your employer.

Strive to be positively recognized.

Be a team player. Be willing to help. Know the goals of your job and how your job fits into the overall organization. Avoid a know-it-all attitude. Try to fit in with the team. Keep your sense of humor.

## FINAL THOUGHTS

In today's world, a job search isn't usually a one-time event in most people's work life. Studies show that the average person will change jobs more frequently than in the past. People used to believe once they had secured a job with good pay and benefits, they would stay 20 to 30 years to retirement, but this is rarely true anymore.

The change is due, in part, to the fluctuating economy and fast-paced technological and scientific advances combined with international competition. That's why it's so important to learn job search techniques and to consider them an invaluable and evolving lifetime skill. Job search skills need to be constantly maintained and updated throughout your work life — even when you're employed. After you get a job you should maintain the following traits:

- Keep your options open. See what your job skills are worth in the job market.
- Get the training or experience you will need to move up or out.
- Keep a list of awards, accomplishments and recognitions to present to your supervisor to lobby for a raise or promotion.

Layoffs and downsizings, after all, can come unexpectedly. That's why it's important to remain updated and networked in your profession even when times are good. While you do not want to have a job and then live in constant fear that it will be taken away, you may want to remain on alert by keeping your skill set and your network current because the future is unpredictable. As Yogi Berra once said: "It's tough to make predictions, especially about the future."

# ENDNOTES: Thank You Notes

The following are examples you can use as templates in different hiring situations.

## THANK YOU LETTER SAMPLE

Your Name
(Address/phone/email)

August 24, 20__

Mr. James Business
Human Resource Manager
ABC Company
111 Employment Way
Anytown, MN 55555

Dear Mr. Business:

Our conversation on August 24 gave me a better understanding of ABC Company and the requirements of the administrative assistant position. The additional information provided by Max and Katherine helped me gain a more complete perspective of the company's values and the job requirement. ABC clearly values positive and highly motivated employees, which are both qualities that I would bring to the job.

As my resume demonstrates, I have strong office and interpersonal skills, have proficiency with the software you use and enjoy the customer service experience you require. I am certain I can make a significant contribution to your company based on my past success as a detail- and results-oriented professional.

Meeting the office staff and touring the facility also reinforced my enthusiasm for this position. I would consider it a privilege to join your team and look forward to hearing your hiring decision. Thank you for the opportunity to discuss my potential for the administrative assistant position at your company. Please contact me if you have any additional questions.

Sincerely,

Your Name

## THANK YOU NOTE SAMPLES

February 28, 20__

Dear Ms. Smith,

It was a pleasure meeting you and Mr. Jones during our interview on Tuesday morning. Lourd's Industries sounds like the perfect place for me to apply my skills, especially since you use the WXY system, the same system I have been supporting the past three years. My proven track record and accomplishments with cost-effective systems can be an asset to your company.

Thank you for considering me for the accounting position. I will contact you by Tuesday of next week to learn of your decision. I look forward to the possibility of joining your staff.

Sincerely,

---

July 28, 20__

Dear Mr. Jones,

Based on our conversation this morning, my interest in working for Luke Industries is stronger than ever. The more I learn about Luke Industries, the more confident I am my skills can add to your company's success. Thank you for the opportunity to interview for the accounting position. I will contact you by Tuesday of next week to learn of your decision.

Sincerely,

# RESPONSE TO REJECTION LETTER SAMPLE

Neda Job
Rural Route 1
Frostbite Falls, MN 55555
June 2, 20__


I. M. Boss
Human Resources Manager
Legitimate Business Services
123 Pinnacle Heights
Lake Wobegon, MN 55555

Dear Ms. Boss:

Thank you for the letter regarding your hiring decision for the
bookkeeping position. I was looking forward to joining your growing
company, and I am disappointed to hear your decision was not in my
favor at this time. I hope you will keep my qualifications in mind for any
future positions as bookkeeper or other related jobs.

Thank you again for your consideration, time and response. I hope
we will have the opportunity to connect again in the near future. Best
wishes on your upcoming sales.

Sincerely,

Neda Job

# KEY JOB-HUNTING WEBSITES AND SOURCES

T he following websites and sources provide valuable information that you can use in your job search. They include job listings, Minnesota WorkForce Center locations, career and education information, and occupational data.

## MINNESOTA CAREER SITES

### MINNESOTAWORKS.NET
**www.MinnesotaWorks.net**

The state's no-fee online job bank uses innovative matching technology to match your resume to job listings. Search the largest job bank in Minnesota 24 hours a day, seven days a week.

### MINNESOTA WORKFORCE CENTERS
**www.mn.gov/deed/wfc**

The Minnesota Department of Employment and Economic Development sponsors about 50 WorkForce Centers where unemployed Minnesotans can receive job search assistance, including jobs data and classes on resume writing and interviewing. A list of the WorkForce Centers and career information are available at the agency's website.

### ISEEK
**www.iseek.org**

Sponsored by a Minnesota public/private partnership, the site lists jobs and offers career and educational information.

### CRAIGSLIST
**www.craigslist.com**

This famous grab bag of community information and sales includes job sections for the Twin Cities, Mankato, Fargo/Moorhead, Brainerd, Bemidji, Rochester, St. Cloud, Duluth and southwest Minnesota.

### JOBS HQ
**www.jobshq.com/**

Jobs HQ has job listings for four states: Minnesota, South Dakota, North Dakota and Wisconsin.

## MINNESOTA CAREER SITES (CONTINUED)

### LEAGUE OF MINNESOTA CITIES

**www.lmc.org/page/1/careers.jsp**

The League of Minnesota Cities has a good list of openings in municipalities around Minnesota.

### JOB-HUNT.ORG

**www.job-hunt.org/jobs/minnesota.shtml**

This is a national site with a useful Minnesota subsection that links to many sites.

### MINNESOTAJOBS.COM

**www.minnesotajobs.com**

The site matches employers with employees in the state. It's free for job seekers and allows people to upload resumes.

### MINNEAPOLIS STAR TRIBUNE

**www.startribune.com**

The state's largest newspaper and online news provider has an active jobs site.

### ST. PAUL PIONEER PRESS

**www.twincities.com**

The Pioneer Press online site has plenty of ads for different professions.

## NATIONAL CAREER SITES

### CAREERONESTOP

**www.careeronestop.org**

Sponsored by the U.S. Department of Labor, the site offers tools to help job seekers, students, businesses and career professionals.

### O*NET

**www.onetcenter.org/**

O*NET Resource Center offers occupational information, career exploration tools and links to help students, job seekers and veterans.

## GENERAL JOB SITES

**CAREER BUILDER**
www.careerbuilder.com

**EMPLOYMENT 911**
www.employment911.com

**INDEED**
www.indeed.com

**JOB.COM**
www.job.com

**US.JOBS**
http://us.jobs/

**JOBDIG**
www.jobdig.com

**NATIONJOB**
www.nationjob.com

**MONSTER**
www.monster.com

**SIMPLY HIRED**
www.SimplyHired.com

Editor's Note: These and other websites cited in Creative Job Search are current as of press time. We recognize that new websites are continuously being created, and we encourage readers to pursue new sources of information as a part of their job search strategy.